GIRL FROM THE MARSH CROFT

and other stories by

SELMA LAGERLÖF

selected and edited by Greta Anderson

Penfield
Press

Stories included in this volume are taken from *The Girl from the Marsh Croft*, translated into English in 1910 by Velma Swanston Howard, and published by Little, Brown and Company; with the exception of "A Story from Halstanäs," "The Peace of God," and "The Brothers" which are from a 1916 edition of *From a Swedish Homestead*, translated by Jessie Brochner and published by Doubleday, Page & Company.

Greta Anderson selected works of Selma Lagerlöf included in *Invisible Links,* a Penfield Press publication of stories by Selma Lagerlöf. She graduated from Stanford University, and received a Ph.D. from Rutgers University. She recently graduated from the Writers' Workshop, University of Iowa.

John Z. Lofgren is executive director of the Greater Lafayette Museum of Art, Lafayette, Indiana, and earlier served as executive director of the American Swedish Institute in Minneapolis. Born in Sweden, he studied in the United States, earning a Ph.D. in the History of Art at the University of Oregon in Eugene. He has written and lectured extensively on Scandinavian art, has coordinated television and radio programs in America and Sweden, and two national festivals: Scandinavia Today (1982-83) and Sweden (1988). In 1987, he was named Officer of the Royal Order of the Polar Star, an honor bestowed by the King of Sweden.

Associate Editors: Jean Caris-Osland, Dorothy Crum, Diane Heusinkveld, John Johnson, Joan Liffring-Zug, Dana Lumby, Robin Ouren, and John D. Zug.

Cover design by Robin Loughran.
Photos courtesy of the Swedish Information Service. Photo of Mårbacka by Walter Pöppel.

Titles by Selma Lagerlöf available from Penfield Press:
POSTPAID *(1996 prices subject to change.)*

   Girl from the Marsh Croft $14.95
   Three Stories: Scandinavian Kings and Queens
        Astrid, Sigrid Storräde, The Silver Mine $12.95
   Memories of Mårbacka $16.95
   Invisible Links $14.95

For a complete list of all titles, please send $2 to:
Penfield Press, 215 Brown Street, Iowa City, Iowa 52245

ISBN 1-57216-014-4 Library of Congress Number 95-69798

PREFACE

Together with August Strindberg (1849-1912), Selma Lagerlöf (1858-1940) is probably the most well-known literary figure to have come out of Sweden. During her lifetime her stories and novels were read and enjoyed all over the world, particularly after she became the first woman to receive the prestigious Nobel Prize in Literature in 1909. Unfortunately, her recognition as a world-famous author has diminished and become overshadowed by modern trends dominating the hectic and chaotic lifestyles of the late 20th century. The essence of Lagerlöf's writings is certainly just as relevant today, however. Her works have powerful imagery and themes that make them universal and timeless. Also, as an avid supporter of causes such as women's rights and world peace, her thoughts and concerns are equally valid today.

Selma Lagerlöf was born in the ancestral manor home of Mårbacka, in the province of Värmland in Sweden. Her childhood was marked by an illness that forced her to avoid strenuous activities but which opened up a world of stories and books instead. Of particular importance for her development as an author was the abundance of family legends and regional tales that her grandmother passed on to her, as well as the rich tradition of Nordic stories and mythology that surrounded her. It was a fantastic fairy tale world, in the midst of reality, that later came to have a great effect on her storytelling.

Lagerlöf was a schoolteacher and wrote fiction on the side for ten years before she was able to support herself solely with her writing. Her first novel, *Gösta Berling's Saga,* published in 1891, did not immediately get the enthusiastic reception it deserved. With its stylistic lightness and emphasis on supernatural events, it caused more wonder than admiration among an audience that was used to the more realistic presentation of the sober 1880s. As time went by, however, many of the leading literary critics came to realize its significance and hailed it as the foremost example of Swedish regional writing. Spurred by this acceptance, Lagerlöf compiled many of her earlier short stories into a collection in 1894 under the heading *Invisible Links*. Using her personal narrative technique, even somewhat reminiscent of the old Icelandic tales, she depicts the Swedish people, their lives and struggles, through glimpses into their souls. The profound truth that comes across in her stories is the fact that people do not act according to opinions or principles, but are driven by inner irrational forces. Thus, in all our confrontations in life, our actions are always unpredictable.

To the American audience, Selma Lagerlöf is perhaps best known and loved for her charming and imaginative storybooks *The Wonderful Adventures of Nils* and *The Further Adventures of Nils,* originally written in 1906-7 as texts for teaching Sweden's geography to schoolchildren.

It is exciting that Penfield Press has taken the initiative to reintroduce the writings of this acclaimed Scandinavian author. Her 1908 collection, *"The Girl from the Marsh Croft,"* continues her storytelling focus on the common people of Sweden.

— John Lofgren, Ph.D.

CONTENTS

*Selma Lagerlöf in the library
at Mårbacka, her ancestral home.*

INTRODUCTION

Selma Lagerlöf's 1908 collection of short stories, *Girl from the Marsh Croft,* reflects the wisdom of one of her characters — that "there must be both light and dark shades in the weaving." Each story is guided by an ideal of "poetic justice," whether it be darkly supernatural or romantically uplifting. This quality makes her stories as satisfying when they end, as they are engaging in their beginnings and middles. Taken together they also express a country ethos, favoring the woods and streams, the hills, and the small-town ways of her youth to the "gray stone streets" and "gray stone walls" of the Stockholm cityscape.

In the title novella of the collection, the self-sacrificing love of a servant girl penetrates the moral fog of the landed gentry to become a guiding ray for all. "The Airship" counters this hopeful message with a harrowing image of destruction wrought by a man who let his musical talent fall by the wayside. Likewise, "The Wedding March" and "The Musician" dramatize the gift of musicianship and the need to honor this gift in humility.

In "The Christmas Rose," Lagerlöf adapts a traditional folk tale motif to one of her favorite Christian themes: the importance of reaching out to society's outcasts. This story, as well as "The Peace of God," was commissioned by a Swedish journal seeking stories for its Christmas edition. Finally, "The Story of a Story" tells how Lagerlöf came to compose her first novel and first received recognition for her writing.

— Greta Anderson, Ph.D.

The Girl from the Marsh Croft

It took place in the courtroom of a rural district. At the head of the judges' table sits an old judge—a tall and massively built man with a broad, rough-hewn visage. For several hours he has been engaged in deciding one case after another, and finally something like disgust and melancholy has taken hold of him. It is difficult to know if it is the heat and closeness of the courtroom that are torturing him, or if he has become low-spirited from handling all these petty wrangles, which seem to spring from no other cause than to bear witness to people's quarrel-mania, uncharitableness, and greed.

He has just begun on one of the last cases to be tried during the day. It concerns a plea for help in the rearing of a child.

This case had already been tried at the last court session, and the protocols of the former suit are being read; therefore one learns that the plaintiff is a poor farmer's daughter and the defendant is a married man.

Moreover, it says in the protocol, the defendant maintains that the plaintiff has unjustly, and only with the desire of profiting thereby, sued the defendant. He admits that at one time the plaintiff had been employed in his household, but that during her stay in his home he had not carried on any way with her, and she has no right to demand assistance from him. The plaintiff still holds firmly to her claim, and after a few witnesses have been heard, the defendant is called to take the oath and show cause why he should not be sentenced by the court to assist the plaintiff.

Both parties have come up and are standing, side by side, before the judges' table. The plaintiff is very young and looks frightened to death. She is weeping from shyness and with difficulty wipes away the tears with a crumpled handkerchief, which she doesn't seem to know how to open out. She wears black clothes, which are quite new and whole, but they fit so badly that one is tempted to think she has borrowed them in order to appear before the Court of Justice in a befitting manner.

As regards the defendant, one sees at a glance that he is a prosperous man. He is about forty and has a bold and dashing appearance. As he stands before the court, he has a very good bearing. One can see that he does not think it a pleasure to stand there, but he doesn't appear to be the least concerned about it.

As soon as the protocols have been read, the judge turns to the defendant and asks him if he holds fast to his denials and if he is prepared to take the oath.

To these questions the defendant answers a curt yes. He digs down in his vest pocket and takes out a statement from the clergyman who attests that he understands the meaning and import of the oath and is qualified to take it.

All through this the plaintiff has been weeping. She appears to be unconquerably bashful, and doggedly keeps her eyes fixed upon the floor. Thus far she has not raised her eyes sufficiently to look the defendant in the face.

As he utters his "yes," she starts back. She moves a step or two nearer the court, as if she had something to say to the contrary, and then she stands there perplexed. It is hardly possible she seems to say to herself; he cannot have answered yes. I have heard wrongly.

Meanwhile the judge takes the clergyman's paper and motions to the court officer. The latter goes up to the table to find the Bible, which lies hidden under a pile of records, and lays it down in front of the defendant.

The plaintiff hears that someone is walking past her and becomes restless. She forces herself to raise her eyes just enough to cast a glance over the table, and she sees then how the court officer moves the Bible.

Again it appears as though she wished to raise some

objection, and again she controls herself. It isn't possible that he will be allowed to take the oath. Surely the judge must prevent him!

The judge is a wise man and knows how people in her home district think and feel. He knows, very likely, how severe all people are as soon as there is anything which affects the marriage relation. They knew of no worse sin than the one she had committed. Would she ever have confessed anything like this about herself if it were not true? The judge must understand the awful contempt that she has brought down upon herself, and not contempt only, but all sorts of misery. No one wanted her in service—no one wanted her work. Her own parents could scarcely tolerate her presence in their cabin and talked all the while of casting her out. Oh, the judge must know that she would never have asked for help from a married man had she no right to it.

Surely the judge could not believe that she had lied in a case like this; that she would have called down upon herself such a terrible misfortune if she had had anyone else to accuse than a married man. And if he knows this, he must stop the oath-taking.

She sees that the judge reads through the clergyman's statements a couple of times and she begins to think he intends to interfere.

True, the judge has a wary look. Now he shifts his glance to the plaintiff, and with that his weariness and disgust become even more marked. It appears as though he were unfavorably disposed toward her. Even if the plaintiff is telling the truth, she is nevertheless a bad woman and the judge cannot feel any sympathy for her.

Sometimes the judge interposes in a case, like a good and wise counselor, and keeps the parties from ruining themselves entirely. But today he is tired and cross and thinks only of letting the legal process have its course.

He lays down the clergyman's recommendation and says a few words to the defendant to the effect that he hopes he has carefully considered the consequences of a perjured oath. The defendant listens to him with the calm air which he has shown all the while, and he answers respectfully and not without dignity.

The plaintiff listens to this in extreme terror. She makes a few vehement protests and wrings her hands. Now she wants to speak to the court. She struggles frightfully with her shyness and with the sobs which prevent her speaking. The result is that she cannot get out an audible word.

Then the oath will be taken! She must give it up. No one will prevent him from swearing away his soul.

Until now, she could not believe this possible. But now she is seized with the certainty that it is close at hand—that it will occur the next second. A fear more overpowering than any she has hitherto felt takes possession of her. She is absolutely paralyzed. She does not even weep more. Her eyes are glazed. It is his intention, then, to bring down upon himself eternal punishment.

She comprehends that he wants to swear himself free for the sake of his wife. But even if the truth were to make trouble in his home, he should not for that reason throw away his soul's salvation.

There is nothing so terrible as perjury. There is something uncanny and awful about that sin. There is no mercy or condonation for it. The gates of the infernal regions open of their own accord when the perjurer's name is mentioned.

If she had then raised her eyes to his face, she would have been afraid of seeing it stamped with damnation's mark, branded by the wrath of God.

As she stands there and works herself into greater and greater terror, the judge instructs the defendant as to how he must place his fingers on the Bible. Then the judge opens the law book to find the form of the oath.

As she sees him place his fingers on the book, she comes a step nearer, and it appears as though she wished

14

to reach across the table and push his hand away.

But as yet she is restrained by a faint hope. She thinks he will relent now—at the last moment.

The judge has found the place in the law book, and now he begins to administer the oath loudly and distinctly. Then he makes a pause for the defendant to repeat his words. The defendant actually starts to repeat, but he stumbles over the words, and the judge must begin again from the beginning.

Now she can no longer entertain a trace of hope. She knows now that he means to swear falsely—that he means to bring down upon himself the wrath of God, both for this life and for the life to come.

She stands wringing her hands in her helplessness. And it is all her fault because she has accused him! But she was without work; she was starving and freezing; the child came near dying. To whom else should she turn for help? Never had she thought that he would be willing to commit such an execrable sin.

The judge has again administered the oath. In a few seconds the thing will have been done: the kind of thing from which there is no turning back—which can never be retrieved, never blotted out.

Just as the defendant begins to repeat the oath, she rushes forward, sweeps away his outstretched hand, and seizes the Bible.

It is her terrible dread which has finally given her courage. He must not swear away his soul; he must not!

The court officer hastens forward instantly to take the Bible from her and to bring her to order. She has a boundless fear of all that pertains to a Court of Justice and actually believes that what she has just done will bring her to prison, but she does not let go her hold on the Bible. Cost what it may, he cannot take the oath. He who would swear also runs up to take the Bible, but she resists him too.

"You shall not take the oath!" she cries, "you shall not!"

This naturally awakens the greatest surprise. The

court attendants elbow their way up to the bar, the jurymen start to rise, the recording clerk jumps up with the ink bottle in his hand to prevent its being upset.

Then the judge shouts in a loud and angry tone, "Silence!" and everybody stands perfectly still.

"What is the matter with you? What business have you with the Bible?" the judge asks the plaintiff in the same hard and severe tone.

Since, with the courage of despair, she has been able to give utterance to her distress, her anxiety has decreased so that she can answer, "He must not take the oath!"

"Be silent, and put back the book!" demands the judge.

She does not obey, but holds the book tightly with both hands. "He cannot take the oath!" she cries fiercely.

"Are you so determined to win your suit?" asks the judge sharply.

"I want to withdraw the suit," she shrieks in a high, shrill voice. "I don't want to force him to swear."

"What are you shrieking about?" demands the judge. "Have you lost your senses?"

She catches her breath suddenly and tries to control herself. She hears herself how she is shrieking. The judge will think she has gone mad if she cannot say what she would say calmly. She struggles with herself again to get control of her voice, and this time she succeeds. She says slowly, earnestly, and clearly, as she looks the judge in the face: "I wish to withdraw the suit. He is the father of the child. I am still fond of him. I don't wish him to swear falsely."

She stands erect and resolute, facing the judges' table, all the while looking the judge square in the face. He sits with both hands resting on the table and for a long while does not take his eyes off her. While the judge is looking at her, a great change comes over him. All the ennui and displeasure in his face vanishes, and the large, roughhewn visage becomes beautiful with the most beautiful emotion. "Ah, see!" he thinks—"Ah, see! such is the mettle of my

16

people. I shall not be vexed at them when there is so much love and godliness even in one of the humblest."

Suddenly the judge feels his eyes fill up with tears; then he pulls himself together, almost ashamed, and casts a hasty glance about him. He sees that the clerks and bailiffs and the whole long row of jurymen are leaning forward and looking at the girl who stands before the judges' table with the Bible hugged close to her. And he sees a light in their faces, as though they had seen something very beautiful, which had made them happy all the way into their souls.

Then the judge casts a glance over the spectators, and he sees that they all breathe a quick sigh of relief, as if they had just heard what they had longed above everything to hear.

Finally, the judge looks at the defendant. Now it is *he* who stands with lowered head and looks at the floor.

The judge turns once more to the poor girl. "It shall be as you wish," he says. "The case shall be stricken from the calendar,"—this to the recording clerk.

The defendant makes a move, as though he wished to interpose an objection. "Well, what now?" the judge bellows at him. "Have you anything against it?"

The defendant's head hangs lower and lower, and he says, almost inaudibly, "Oh, no, I dare say it is best to let it go that way."

The judge sits still a moment more, and then he pushes the heavy chair back, rises, and walks around the table and up to the plaintiff.

"Thank you!" he says and gives her his hand. She has laid down the Bible and stands wiping away the tears with the crumpled up handkerchief.

"Thank you!" says the judge once more, taking her hand and shaking it as if it belonged to a real man's man.

17

II

Let no one imagine that the girl who had passed through such a trying ordeal at the bar of justice thought that she had done anything praiseworthy! On the contrary, she considered herself disgraced before the whole courtroom. She did not understand that there was something honorable in the fact that the judge had gone over and shaken hands with her. She thought it simply meant that the trial was over and that she might go her way.

Nor did she observe that people gave her kindly glances and that there were several who wanted to press her hand. She stole by and wanted only to go. There was a crush at the door. The court session was over and many in their hurry to get out made a rush for the door. She drew aside and was about the last person to leave the courtroom because she felt that everyone else ought to go before her.

When she finally came out, Gudmund Erlandsson's cart stood in waiting at the door. Gudmund was seated in the cart, holding the reins, and was apparently waiting for someone. As soon as he saw her among all the people who poured out of the courtroom, he called to her: "Come here, Helga! You can ride with me since we are going in the same direction."

Although she heard her name, she could not believe that it was she whom he was calling. It was not possible that Gudmund Erlandsson wanted to ride with her. He was the most attractive man in the whole parish, young and handsome and of good family connections and popular with everyone. She could not imagine that he wished to associate with her.

She was walking with the head shawl drawn far down on her forehead, and was hastening past him without either glancing up or answering.

"Don't you hear, Helga, that you can ride with me?" said Gudmund, and there was a friendly note in his voice.

But she couldn't grasp that Gudmund meant well by her. She thought that, in one way or another, he wished to make sport of her and was only waiting for those who stood nearby to begin tittering and laughing. She cast a frightened and indignant glance at him, and almost ran from the courthouse grounds to be out of earshot when the laughter should start in.

Gudmund was unmarried at that time and lived at home with his parents. His father was a farm owner. His was not a large farm and he was not rich, but he made a good living. The son had gone to the courthouse to fetch some deeds for his father, but as there was also another purpose in the trip, he had groomed himself carefully. He had taken the brand new trap with not a crack in the lacquering, had rubbed up the harness and curried the horse until he shone like satin. He had placed a bright red blanket on the seat beside him, and himself he had adorned with a short hunting jacket, a small gray felt hat, and top boots, into which the trousers were tucked. This was no holiday attire, but he probably knew that he looked handsome and manly.

Gudmund was seated alone in the cart when he drove from home in the morning, but he had agreeable things to think of and the time had not seemed long to him. When he had arrived about half-way, he came across a poor young girl who was walking very slowly and looked as though she were scarcely able to move her feet because of exhaustion. It was autumn and the road was rain-soaked, and Gudmund saw how, with every step, she sank deeper into the mud. He stopped and asked where she was going. When he learned that she was on her way to the courthouse, he invited her to ride. She thanked him and stepped up on the back of the cart to the narrow board where the hay sack was tied, as though she dared not touch the red blanket beside Gudmund. Nor was it his meaning that she should sit beside him. He didn't know who she was, but he supposed her to be the daughter of some poor backwoodsman and thought the rear of the cart was quite good enough for her.

When they came to a steep hill and the horse began to slow up, Gudmund started talking. He wanted to know her name and where she was from. When he learned that her name was Helga, and that she came from a backwoods farm called Big Marsh, he began to feel uneasy. "Have you always lived at home on the farm or have you been out to service?" he asked.

The past year she had been at home, but before this she had been working out.

"Where?" asked Gudmund hastily.

He thought it was a long while before the answer was forthcoming. "At the West Farm, with Per Mårtensson," she said finally, sinking her voice as if she would rather not have been heard.

But Gudmund heard her. "Indeed! Then it is you who—" said he, but did not conclude his meaning. He turned from her, and sat up straight in his seat and said not another word to her.

Gudmund gave the horse rap upon rap and talked loudly to himself about the wretched condition of the road and was in a very bad humor.

The girl sat still for a moment; presently Gudmund felt her hand upon his arm. "What do you wish?" he asked without turning his head.

Oh, he was to stop, so she could jump out.

"Why so?" sneered Gudmund. "Aren't you riding comfortably?"

"Yes, thank you, but I prefer to walk."

Gudmund struggled a little with himself. It was provoking that he should have bidden a person of Helga's sort to ride with him today of all days! But he thought also that since he had taken her into the wagon, he could not drive her out.

"Stop, Gudmund!" said the girl once again. She spoke in a very decided tone, and Gudmund drew in the reins.

"It is she, of course, who wishes to step down," thought he. "I don't have to force her to ride against her will."

She was down on the road before the horse had time to stop. "I thought you knew who I was when you asked me to ride," she said, "or I should not have stepped into the cart."

Gudmund muttered a short good-bye and drove on. She was doubtless right in thinking that he knew her. He had seen the girl from the marsh croft many times as a child, but she had changed since she was grown up. At first he was very glad to be rid of the traveling companion, but gradually he began to feel displeased with himself. He could hardly have acted differently, yet he did not like being cruel to anyone.

Shortly after Gudmund had parted from Helga, he turned out of the road and up a narrow street, and came to a large and fine estate. As Gudmund drew up before the gate, the house door opened and one of the daughters appeared.

Gudmund raised his hat; at the same time a faint flush covered his face. "Wonder if the juryman is at home?" said he.

"No, Father has gone down to the courthouse," replied the daughter.

"Oh, then he has already gone," said Gudmund. I drove over to ask if the juryman would ride with me. I'm going to the courthouse."

"Father is always so punctual!" bewailed the daughter.

"It doesn't matter," said Gudmund.

"Father would have been pleased, I dare say, to ride behind such a fine horse and in such a pretty cart as you have," remarked the girl pleasantly.

Gudmund smiled a little when he heard this commendation.

"Well, then, I must be off again," said he.

"Won't you step in, Gudmund?"

"Thank you, Hildur, but I'm going to the courthouse,

you know. It won't do for me to be late."

Then Gudmund took the direct road to the courthouse. He was very well pleased with himself and thought no more of his meeting with Helga. It was fortunate that only Hildur had come out on the porch and that she had seen the cart and blanket, the horse and harness. She had probably taken note of everything.

This was the first time Gudmund had attended a court. He thought that there was much to see and learn, and remained the whole day. He was sitting in the courtroom when Helga's case came up; he saw how she snatched the Bible and hugged it close, and saw how she defied both court attendants and judge. When it was all over and the judge had shaken hands with Helga, Gudmund rose quickly and went out. He hurriedly hitched the horse to the cart and drove up to the steps. He thought Helga had been brave, and now he wished to honor her. But she was so frightened that she did not understand his purpose, and stole away from his intended honor.

The same day Gudmund came to the marsh croft late in the evening. It was a little croft, which lay at the base of the forest ridge that enclosed the parish. The road leading to it was passable only by horse in winter, and Gudmund had to go there on foot. It was difficult for him to find his way. He came near breaking his legs on stumps and stones, and he had to wade through brooks which crossed the path in several places. Had it not been for the bright moonlight, he could not have found his way to the croft. He thought it was a very hard road that Helga had to tramp this day.

The croft at Big Marsh lay on the clearing about half-way up the ridge. Gudmund had never been there before, but he had often seen the place from the valley and was sufficiently familiar with it to know that he had gone aright.

All around the clearing lay a hedge of brushwood, which was very thick and difficult to get through. It was

22

probably meant to be a kind of defense and protection against the whole wilderness that surrounded the croft. The cabin stood at the upper edge of the enclosure. Before it stretched a sloping house-yard covered with short, thick grass; and below the yard lay a couple of gray outhouses and a larder with a moss-covered roof. It was a poor and humble place, but one couldn't deny that it was picturesque up there. The marsh, from which the croft had derived its name, lay somewhere near and sent forth mists which rose, beautiful, splendid, and silvery, in the moonlight, forming a halo around the marsh. The highest peak of the mountain loomed above the mist, and the ridge, prickly with pines, was sharply outlined against the horizon. Over the valley shone the moon. It was so light that one could distinguish fields and orchards and a winding brook, over which the mists curled, like the faintest smoke. It was not very far down there, but the peculiar thing was that the valley lay like a world apart, with which the forest and all that belonged to it seemed to have nothing in common. It was as if the people who lived here in the forest must ever remain under the shadow of these trees. They might find it quite as hard to feel contented down in the valley as woodcock and eagle-owl and lynx and star-flowers.

Gudmund tramped across the open grass plot and up to the cabin. There a gleam of firelight streamed through the windows; he peeped into the cabin to see if Helga was there. A small lamp burned on the table near the window, and there sat the master of the house, mending old shoes. The mistress was seated farther back in the room, close to the fireplace, where a slow fire burned. The spinning wheel was before her, but she had paused in her work to play with a little child. She had taken it up from the cradle, and Gudmund heard how she prattled to it. Her face was lined and wrinkled and she looked severe. But, as she bent over the child, she had a mild expression and smiled as tenderly at the little one as his own mother might have.

Gudmund peered in, but could not see Helga in any corner of the cabin. Then he thought it was best to remain outside until she came. He was surprised that she had not reached home. Perhaps she had stopped on the way somewhere to see an acquaintance and to get some food and rest? At all events, she would have to come back soon if she wished to be indoors before it was very late at night.

Gudmund stood still a moment and listened for footsteps. He thought that never before had he sensed such stillness. It was as though the whole forest held its breath and stood waiting for something extraordinary to happen.

No one tramped in the forest, no branch was broken, and no stone rolled down.

"Surely, Helga won't be long in coming! I wonder what she will say when she sees that I'm here?" thought Gudmund. "Perhaps she will scream and rush into the forest and will not dare come home the whole night!"

At the same time, it struck him as rather strange that now, all of a sudden, he had so much business with that marsh croft girl!

On his return from the courthouse to his home, he had, as usual, gone to his mother to relate his experiences of the day. Gudmund's mother was a sensible and broad-minded woman who had always understood how to treat her son, and he had as much confidence in her now as when he was a child. She had been an invalid for several years and could not walk, but sat all day in her chair. It was always a good hour for her when Gudmund came home from an outing and brought her the news.

When Gudmund had told his mother about Helga from Big Marsh, he observed that she became thoughtful. For a long while she sat quietly and looked straight ahead. "There seems to be something good in that girl still," she remarked. "It will never do to condemn a person because she has once met with misfortune. She might be very grateful to anyone who helped her now."

Gudmund apprehended at once what his mother was

24

thinking of. She could no longer help herself, but must have someone near her continually, and it was always difficult to find anybody who cared to remain in that capacity. His mother was exacting and not easy to get on with, and, moreover, all young folk preferred other work where they could have more freedom. Now, it must have occurred to his mother that she ought to take Helga from Big Marsh into her service, and Gudmund thought this a capital idea. Helga would certainly be very devoted to his mother.

"It will be hard for the child," remarked the mother after a little, and Gudmund understood that she was thinking seriously of the matter.

"Surely the parents would let it stay with them?" said Gudmund.

"It does not follow that she wants to part with it."

"She will have to give up thinking of what she wants or doesn't want. I thought that she looked starved out. They can't have much to eat at the croft," said the son.

To this his mother made no reply, but began to talk of something else. It was evident that some new misgivings had come to her, which hindered her from coming to a decision.

Then Gudmund told her of how he had found a pretext for calling at the juryman's at Älvåkra and had met Hildur. He mentioned what she had said of the horse and wagon, and it was easily seen that he was pleased with the meeting. His mother was also very much pleased. Where she sat in the cottage, unable to move from her chair, it was her constant occupation to spin plans for her son's future, and it was she who had first hit upon the idea that he should try and set his cap for the pretty daughter of the juryman. It was the finest match he could make.

The juryman was a yeoman farmer. He owned the largest farm in the parish and had much money and power. It was really absurd to hope that he would be satisfied with a son-in-law with no more wealth than

Gudmund, but it was also possible that he would conform to his daughter's wishes. That Gudmund could win Hildur if he so wished, his mother was certain.

This was the first time Gudmund had betrayed to his mother that her thought had taken root in him, and they talked long of Hildur and of all the riches and advantages that would come to the chosen one. Soon there was another lull in the conversation, for his mother was again absorbed in her thoughts. "Couldn't you send for this Helga? I should like to see her before taking her into my service," said the mother finally.

"It is well, Mother, that you wish to take her under your wing," remarked Gudmund, thinking to himself that if his mother had a nurse with whom she was satisfied, his wife would have a more pleasant life here. "You'll see that you will be pleased with the girl," he continued.

"Then, too, it would be a good deed to take her in hand," added the mother. As it grew dusk, the invalid retired, and Gudmund went out to the stable to tend the horses. It was beautiful weather, with a clear atmosphere, and the whole tract lay bathed in moonlight. It occurred to him that he ought to go to Big Marsh tonight and convey his mother's greeting. If the weather should continue clear on the morrow, he would be so busy taking in oats that neither he nor anyone else would find time to go there.

Now that Gudmund was standing outside the cabin at Big Marsh croft listening, he certainly heard no footsteps. But there were other sounds which at short intervals pierced through the stillness. He heard a soft weeping, a very low and smothered moaning, with now and then a sob. Gudmund thought that the sounds came from the outhouse lane, and he walked toward it. As he was nearing, the sobs ceased; but it was evident that someone moved in the woodshed. Gudmund seemed to comprehend instantly who was there. "Is it you, Helga, who sits here and weeps?" asked Gudmund, placing himself in the doorway so that the girl could not rush away before he had spoken.

Again it was perfectly still. Gudmund had guessed rightly that it was Helga who sat there and wept; but she tried to smother the sobs, so that Gudmund would think he had heard wrongly and go away. It was pitch dark in the woodshed, and she knew that he could not see her.

But Helga was in such despair that evening, it was not easy for her to keep back the sobs. She had not as yet gone into the cabin to see her parents. She hadn't had the courage to go in. When she trudged up the steep hill in the light and thought of how she must tell her parents that she was not to receive any assistance from Per Mårtensson in the rearing of her child, she began to fear all the harsh and cruel things she felt they would say to her and thought of burying herself in the swamp. And in her terror, she jumped up and tried to rush past Gudmund, but he was too alert for her.

"Oh no! You shan't get by before I have spoken with you."

"Only let me go!" she said, looking wildly at him.

"You look as though you wanted to jump into the river," said he; for now she was out in the moonlight and he could see her face.

"Well, what matters it if I did?" said Helga, throwing her head back and looking him straight in the eye. "This morning you didn't even care to have me ride on the back of your cart. No one wants to have anything to do with me! You must surely understand that it is best for a miserable creature like me to put an end to herself."

Gudmund did not know what to do next. He wished himself far away, but he thought, also, that he could not desert a person who was in such distress. "Listen to me. Only promise that you will listen to what I have to say to you; afterwards you may go wherever you wish."

She promised.

"Is there anything here to sit on?"

"The chopping block is over yonder."

"Then go over there and sit down and be quiet!"

She went very obediently and seated herself.

"And don't cry any more!" said he, for he thought he was beginning to get control over her. But he should not have said this, for immediately she buried her face in her hands and cried harder than ever.

"Stop crying!" he said, ready to stamp his foot at her. "There are those, I dare say, who are worse off than you are."

"No, no one can be worse off!"

"You are young and strong. You should see how my mother fares! She is so wasted from suffering that she cannot move, but she never complains."

"She is not abandoned by everybody, as I am."

"You are not abandoned, either. I have spoken with my mother about you."

There was a pause in the sobs. One heard, as it were the great stillness of the forest, which always held its breath and waited for something wonderful. "I was to say to you that you should come down to my mother tomorrow that she might see you. Mother thinks of asking if you would care to take service with us."

"Did she think of asking *me*?"

"Yes; but she wants to see you first."

"Does she know that—"

"She knows as much about you as all the rest do."

The girl leaped up with a cry of joy and wonderment, and the next moment Gudmund felt a pair of arms around his neck. He was thoroughly frightened, and his first impulse was to break loose and run, but he calmed himself and stood still. He understood that the girl was so beside herself with joy that she didn't know what she was doing. At that moment she could have hugged the worst ruffian, only to find a little sympathy in the great happiness that had come to her.

"If she will take me into her service, I can live!" said she, burying her head on Gudmund's breast and weeping again. "You may know that I was in earnest when I wished to go down into the swamp," she said. "You deserve thanks for coming. You have saved my life." Until then Gudmund had been standing motionless, but now he felt that something tender and warm was beginning to stir within him. He raised his hand and stroked her hair. Then she started, as if awakened from a dream, and stood up straight as a rod before him. "You deserve thanks for coming," she repeated. She had become flame-red in the face, and he too reddened.

"Well, then, you will come home tomorrow," he said, putting out his hand to say good-bye.

"I shall never forget that you came to me tonight," said Helga, and her great gratitude got the mastery over her shyness.

"Oh, yes, it was well perhaps that I came," he said quite calmly, and he felt rather pleased with himself. "You will go in now, of course?"

"Yes, now I shall go in."

Gudmund suddenly felt himself rather pleased with Helga too—as one usually is with a person whom one has succeeded in helping. She lingered and did not want to go. "I would like to see you safely under shelter before I leave."

"I thought they might retire before I went in."

"No, you must go in at once, so that you can have your supper and rest yourself," said he, thinking it was agreeable to take her in hand.

She went at once to the cabin, and he accompanied her, pleased and proud because she obeyed him.

When she stood on the threshold, they said good-bye to each other again; but before he had gone two paces, she came after him. "Remain just outside the door until I am in. It will be easier for me if I know that you are standing there."

"Yes," said he, "I shall stand here until you have come over the worst of it."

Then Helga opened the cabin door, and Gudmund

noticed that she left it slightly ajar. It was as if she did not wish to feel herself separated from her helper who stood outside. Nor did he feel any compunction about hearing all that happened within the cabin.

The old folks nodded pleasantly to Helga as she came in. Her mother promptly laid the child in the crib, and then went over to the cupboard and brought out a bowl of milk and a bread cake and placed them on the table.

"There! Now sit down and eat," said she. Then she went up to the fireplace and freshened the fire. "I have kept the fire alive, so you could dry your feet and warm yourself when you came home. But eat something first! It is food that you need most."

All the while Helga had been standing at the door. "You mustn't receive me so well, Mother," she said in a low tone. "I will get no money from Per. I have renounced his help."

"There was someone here from the courthouse this evening who had been there and heard how it turned out for you," said the mother. "We know all."

Helga was still standing by the door, looking out, as if she did not know which was in or out.

Then the farmer put down his work, pushed his spectacles up on his forehead, and cleared his throat for a speech of which he had been thinking the whole evening. "It is a fact, Helga," said he, "that Mother and I have always wanted to be decent and honorable folk, but we have thought that we had been disgraced on your account. It was as though we had not taught you to distinguish between good and evil. But when we learned what you did today, we said to each other—Mother and I—that now folks could see anyway that you have had a proper bringing up and right teaching, and we thought that perhaps we might yet be happy in you. And Mother did not want that we should go to bed before you came so that you might have a hearty welcome home."

III

Helga from the marsh croft came to Närlunda, and there all went well. She was willing and teachable and grateful for every kind word said to her. She always felt herself to be the humblest of mortals and never wanted to push herself ahead. It was not long before the household and the servants were satisfied with her.

The first days it appeared as if Gudmund was afraid to speak to Helga. He feared that this croft girl would get notions into her head because he had come to her assistance. But these were needless worries. Helga regarded him as altogether too fine and noble for her even to raise her eyes to. Gudmund soon perceived that he did not have to keep her at a distance. She was more shy of him than of anyone else.

The autumn that Helga came to Närlunda, Gudmund paid many visits to Älvåkra, and there was much talk about the good chance he stood of being the prospective son-in-law of this estate. That the courtship had been successful all were assured at Christmas. Then the juryman, with his wife and daughter, came over to Närlunda, and it was evident that they had come there to see how Hildur would fare if she married Gudmund.

This was the first time that Helga saw, at close range, her whom Gudmund was to marry. Hildur Ericsdotter was not yet twenty, but the marked thing about her was that no one could look at her without thinking what a handsome and dignified mistress she would be some day. She was tall and well-built, fair and pretty, and apparently liked to have many about her to look after. She was never timid; she talked much and seemed to know everything better than the one with whom she was talking. She had attended school in the city for a couple of years and wore the prettiest frocks Helga had ever seen, but yet she did not impress one as being showy or vain. Rich and beautiful as she was, she might have married a gentleman at any time, but she always declared that she did not wish to be a fine lady and sit with folded hands. She wanted to marry a farmer and look after her own house, like a real farmer's wife.

Helga thought Hildur a perfect wonder. Never had she seen anyone who made such a superb appearance. Nor had she ever dreamed that a person could be so nearly perfect in every particular. To her it seemed a great joy that in the near future she was to serve such a mistress.

Everything had gone off well during the juryman's visit. But whenever Helga looked back upon that day, she experienced a certain unrest. It seems that when the visitors had arrived, she had gone around and served coffee. When she came in with the tray, the juryman's wife leaned forward and asked her mistress if she was not the girl from the marsh croft. She did not lower her voice much, and Helga had distinctly heard the question.

Mother Ingeborg answered yes, and then the other had said something which Helga couldn't hear. But it was to the effect that she thought it singular they wanted a person of that sort in the house. This caused Helga many anxious moments. She tried to console herself with the thought that it was not Hildur, but her mother, who had said this.

One Sunday in the early spring, Helga and Gudmund walked home together from church. As they came down the slope, they were with the other church people, but soon one after another dropped off until, finally, Helga and Gudmund were alone.

Then Gudmund happened to think that he had not been alone with Helga since that night at the croft, and the memory of that night came forcibly back to him. He had thought of their first meeting often enough during the winter, and with it he had always felt something sweet and pleasant thrill through his senses. As he went about his work, he would call forth in thought that whole beautiful evening: the white mist, the bright moonlight, the

32

dark forest heights, the light valley, and the girl who had thrown her arms round his neck and wept for joy. The whole incident became more beautiful each time that it recurred to his memory. But when Gudmund saw Helga going about among the others at home, toiling and slaving, it was hard for him to think that it was she who had shared in this. Now that he was walking alone with her on the church slope, he couldn't help wishing for a moment that she would be the same girl she was on that evening.

Helga began immediately to speak of Hildur. She praised her much, saying she was the prettiest and most sensible girl in the whole parish, and congratulated Gudmund because he would have such an excellent wife. "You must tell her to let me remain always at Närlunda," she said. "It will be a pleasure to work for a mistress like her."

Gudmund smiled at her enthusiasm, but answered only in monosyllables, as though he did not exactly follow her. It was well, of course, that she was so fond of Hildur, and so happy because he was going to be married.

"You have been content to be with us this winter?" he asked.

"Indeed I have! I cannot begin to tell you how kind Mother Ingeborg and all of you have been to me!"

"Have you not been homesick for the forest?"

"Oh, yes, in the beginning, but not now any more."

"I thought that one who belonged to the forest could not help yearning for it."

Helga turned half-around and looked at him, who walked on the other side of the road. Gudmund had become almost a stranger to her, but now there was something in his voice, his smile, that was familiar. Yes, he was the same man who had come to her and saved her in her greatest distress. Although he was to marry another, she was certain that he wanted to be a good friend to her, and a faithful helper.

She was very happy to feel that she could confide in

33

him, as in none other, and thought that she must tell him of all that had happened to her since they last talked together. "I must tell you that it was rather hard for me the first weeks at Närlunda," she began. "But you must not speak of this to your mother."

"If you want me to be silent, I'll be silent."

"Fancy! I was so homesick in the beginning that I was about to go back to the forest."

"Were you homesick? I thought you were glad to be with us."

"I simply could not help it," she said apologetically. "I understood, of course, how well it was for me to be here; you were all so good to me, and the work was not so hard but that I could manage with it, but I was homesick nevertheless. There was something that took hold of me and wanted to draw me back to the forest. I thought that I was deserting and betraying someone who had a right to me, when I wanted to stay here in the village."

"It was perhaps—" began Gudmund, but checked himself.

"No, it was not the boy I longed for. I knew that he was well cared for and that mother was kind to him. It was nothing in particular. I felt as though I were a wild bird that had been caged, and I thought I should die if I were not let out."

"To think that you had such a hard time of it!" said Gudmund smiling, for now, all at once, he recognized her. Now it was as if nothing had come between them, but that they had parted at the forest farm the evening before.

Helga smiled again, but continued to speak of her torments. "I didn't sleep a single night," said she, "and as soon as I went to bed, the tears started to flow, and when I got up of a morning, the pillow was wet through. In the daytime, when I went about among all of you, I could keep back the tears, but as soon as I was alone my eyes would fill up."

"You have wept much in your time," said Gudmund

34

without looking the least bit sympathetic as he pronounced the words.

Helga thought that he was laughing to himself all the while. "You surely don't comprehend how hard it was for me!" she said, speaking faster and faster in her effort to make him understand her. "A great longing took possession of me and carried me out of myself. Not for a moment could I feel happy! Nothing was beautiful, nothing was a pleasure; not a human being could I become attached to. You all remained just as strange to me as you were the first time I entered the house."

"But didn't you say a moment ago that you wished to remain with us?" said Gudmund wonderingly.

"Of course I did!"

"Then, surely, you are not homesick now?"

"No, it has passed over. I have been cured. Wait, and you shall hear!"

As she said this, Gudmund crossed to the other side of the road and walked beside her, laughing to himself all the while. He seemed glad to hear her speak, but probably he didn't attach much importance to what she was relating. Gradually Helga took on his mood, and she thought everything was becoming easy and light. The church road was long and difficult to walk, but today she was not tired. There was something that carried her. She continued with her story because she had begun it, but it was no longer of much importance to her to speak. It would have been quite as agreeable to her if she might have walked silently beside him.

"When I was the most unhappy," she said, "I asked Mother Ingeborg one Saturday evening to let me go home and remain over Sunday. And that evening, as I tramped over the hills to the marsh, I believed positively that I should never again go back to Närlunda. But at home Father and Mother were so happy because I had found service with good and respectable people, that I didn't dare tell them I could not endure remaining with you.

35

Then, too, as soon as I came up into the forest all the anguish and pain vanished entirely. I thought the whole thing had been only a fancy. And then it was so difficult about the child. Mother had become attached to the boy and had made him her own. He wasn't mine any more. And it was well thus, but it was hard to get used to."

"Perhaps you began to be homesick for us?" blurted Gudmund.

"Oh, no! On Monday morning, as I awoke and thought of having to return to you, the longing came over me again. I lay crying and fretting because the only right and proper thing for me to do was to go back to Närlunda. But I felt all the same as though I were going to be ill or lose my senses if I went back. Suddenly I remembered having once heard someone say that if one took some ashes from the hearth in one's own home and strewed them on the fire in the strange place, one would be rid of homesickness."

"Then it was a remedy that was easy to take," said Gudmund.

"Yes, but it was supposed to have this effect also: afterwards one could never be content in any other place. If one were to move from the homestead to which one had borne the ashes, one must long to get back there again just as much as one had longed before to get away from there."

"Couldn't one carry ashes along wherever one moved to?"

"No, it can't be done more than once. Afterwards there is no turning back, so it was a great risk to try anything like that."

"I shouldn't have taken chances on a thing of that kind," said Gudmund, and she could hear that he was laughing at her.

"But I dared, all the same," retorted Helga. "It was better than having to appear as an ingrate in your mother's eyes and in yours, when you had tried to help me. I brought a little ashes from home, and when I got back to Närlunda I watched for my opportunity, when no one was

36

in, and scattered the ashes over the hearth."

"And now you believe it is ashes that have helped you?"

"Wait, and you shall hear how it turned out! Immediately I became absorbed in my work and thought no more about the ashes all that day. I grieved exactly as before and was just as weary of everything as I had been. There was much to be done that day, both in the house and out of it, and when I finished with the evening's milking and was going in, the fire on the hearth was already lighted."

"Now I'm very curious to hear what happened," said Gudmund.

"Think! Already, as I was crossing the house yard, I thought there was something familiar in the gleam from the fire, and when I opened the door, it flashed across my mind that I was going into our own cabin and that Father and Mother would be sitting by the hearth. This flew past like a dream, but when I came in, I was surprised that it looked so pretty and home-like in the cottage. To me your mother and the rest of you had never appeared as pleasant as you did in the firelight. It seemed really good to come in, and this was not so before. I was so astonished that I could hardly keep from clapping my hands and shouting. I thought you were all so changed. You were no longer strangers to me and I could talk to you about all sorts of things. You can understand, of course, that I was happy, but I couldn't help being astonished. I wondered if I had been bewitched, and then I remembered the ashes I had strewn over the hearth."

"Yes, it was marvelous," said Gudmund.

He did not believe the least little bit in witchcraft and was not at all superstitious, but he didn't dislike hearing Helga talk of such things. "Now the wild forest girl has returned," thought he. "Can anybody comprehend how one who has passed through all that she has can still be so childish?"

"Of course it was wonderful," said Helga. "And the same thing has been coming back all winter. As soon as the fire on the hearth was burning, I felt the same confidence and security as if I had been at home. But there must be something extraordinary about this fire—not with any other kind of fire, perhaps—only that which burns on a hearth, with all the household gathered around it, night after night. It gets sort of acquainted with one. It plays and dances for one and talks to one, and sometimes it is ill-humored. It is as if it had the power to create comfort and discomfort. I thought now that the fire from home had come to me and that it gave the same glow of pleasure to everyone here that it had done back home."

"What if you had to leave Närlunda?" said Gudmund.

"Then I must long to come back again all my life," said she. And the quiver in her voice betrayed that this was spoken in profound seriousness.

"Well, I shall not be the one to drive you away!" said Gudmund. Although he was laughing, there was something warm in his tone.

They started no new subject of conversation, but walked on in silence until they came to the homestead. Now and then Gudmund turned his head to look at her who was walking at his side. She had gathered strength after her hard time of the year before. Her features were delicate and refined; her hair was like an aureole around her head, and her eyes were not easy to read. Her step was light and elastic, and when she spoke, the words came readily, yet modestly. She was afraid of being laughed at, still she had to speak out what was in her heart.

Gudmund wondered if he wished Hildur to be like this, but he probably didn't. This Helga would be nothing special to marry.

A fortnight later Helga heard that she must leave Närlunda in April because Hildur Ericsdotter would not live under the same roof with her. The master and mistress of the house did not say this in so many words, but the mistress hinted that when the new daughter-in-law came, they would in all probability get so much help from

38

her they would not require so many servants. On another occasion she said she had heard of a good place where Helga would fare better than with them.

It was not necessary for Helga to hear anything further to understand that she must leave, and she immediately announced that she would move, but she did not wish any other situation and would return to her home.

It was apparent that it was not of their own free will they were dismissing Helga from Närlunda.

When she was leaving, there was a spread for her. It was like a party, and Mother Ingeborg gave her such heaps of dresses and shoes that she, who had come to them with only a bundle under her arm, could now barely find room enough in a chest for her possessions.

"I shall never again have such an excellent servant in my house as you have been," said Mother Ingeborg. "And do not think too hard of me for letting you go! You understand, no doubt, that it is not my will, this. I shall not forget you. So long as I have any power, you shall never have to suffer want."

She arranged with Helga that she was to weave sheets and towels for her. She gave her employment for at least half a year.

Gudmund was in the woodshed splitting wood the day Helga was leaving. He did not come in to say good-bye, although his horse was at the door. He appeared to be so busy that he didn't take note of what was going on. She had to go out to him to say farewell.

He laid down the axe, took Helga's hand, and said rather hurriedly, "Thank you for all!" and began chopping again. Helga had wanted to say something about her understanding that it was impossible for them to keep her and that it was all her own fault. She had brought this upon herself. But Gudmund chopped away until the splinters flew around him, and she couldn't make up her mind to speak.

But the strangest thing about this whole moving affair

was that the master himself, old Erland Erlandsson, drove Helga up to the marsh.

Gudmund's father was a little wizened man, with a bald pate and beautiful and knowing eyes. He was very timid, and so reticent at times that he did not speak a word the whole day. So long as everything went smoothly, one took no notice of him, but when anything went wrong, he always said and did what there was to be said and done to right matters. He was a capable accountant and enjoyed the confidence of every man in the township. He executed all kinds of public commissions and was more respected than many a man with a large estate and great riches.

Erland Erlandsson drove Helga home in his own wagon, and he wouldn't allow her to step down and walk up any of the hills. When they arrived at the marsh croft, he sat a long while in the cabin and talked with Helga's parents, telling them of how pleased he and Mother Ingeborg had been with her. It was only because they did not need so many servants that they were sending her home. She, who was the youngest, must go. They had felt that it was wrong to dismiss any of those who were old in their service.

Erland Erlandsson's speech had the desired effect, and the parents gave Helga a warm welcome. When they heard that she had received such large orders that she could support herself with weaving, they were satisfied, and she remained at home.

IV

Gudmund thought that he had loved Hildur until the day when she exacted from him the promise that Helga should be sent away from Närlunda; at least up to that time, there was no one whom he had esteemed more highly than Hildur. No other young girl, to his thinking, could come up to her. It had been a pleasure for him to picture a future with Hildur. They would be rich and looked up to, and he

40

felt instinctively that the home Hildur managed would be good to live in. He liked also to think that he would be well supplied with money after he had married her. He could then improve the land, rebuild all the tumble-down houses, extend the farm, and be a real landed proprietor.

The same Sunday that he had walked home from church with Helga, he had driven over to Älvåkra in the evening. Then Hildur had started talking about Helga and had said that she wouldn't come to Närlunda until that girl was sent away. At first Gudmund had tried to dismiss the whole matter as a jest, but it was soon obvious that Hildur was in earnest. Gudmund pleaded Helga's cause exceedingly well and remarked that she was very young when first sent out to service, and it was not strange that things went badly when she came across such a worthless fellow as Per Mårtensson. But since his mother had taken her in hand, she had always conducted herself well. "It can't be right to push her out," said he. "Then, perhaps, she might meet with misfortune again." But Hildur would not yield. "If that girl is to remain at Närlunda, then I will never come there," she declared. "I cannot tolerate a person of that kind in my home."

"You don't know what you are doing," said Gudmund. "No one understands so well as Helga how to care for Mother. We have all been glad that she came to us. Before she came, Mother was often peevish and depressed."

"I shall not compel you to send her away," said Hildur, but it was clear that if Gudmund were to take her at her word, in this instance, she was ready to break the engagement.

"It will probably have to be as you wish," said Gudmund. He did not feel that he could jeopardize his whole future for Helga's sake, but he was very pale when he acquiesced, and he was silent and low-spirited the entire evening.

It was this which had caused Gudmund to fear that perhaps Hildur was not altogether what he had fancied

41

her. He did not like, I dare say, that she had pitted her will against his. But the worst of it was that he could not comprehend anything else than that she was in the wrong. He felt that he would willingly have given in to her had she been broad-minded, but instead, it seemed to him, she was only petty and heartless. Once his doubts were awakened, it was not long before he perceived one thing and another which were not as he wished. "Doubtless she is one of those who think first and foremost of themselves," he muttered every time he parted from her, and he wondered how long her love for him would last if it were put to the test. He tried to console himself with the idea that all people thought of themselves first, but instantly Helga flashed into his mind. He saw her as she stood in the courtroom and snatched the Bible, and heard how she cried out: "I withdraw the suit. I am still fond of him and I don't want him to swear falsely." It was thus he would have Hildur. Helga had become for him a standard by which he measured people. Though certainly there were many who were equal to her in his affection!

Day by day he thought less of Hildur, but it did not occur to him that he should relinquish his prospective bride. He tried to imagine his discouragement was simply an idle whim. Only a few weeks ago he regarded her as the best in the world!

Had this been at the beginning of the courtship, he would have withdrawn, perhaps, but now the banns were already published and the wedding day fixed, and in his home they had begun repairing and rebuilding. Nor did he wish to forfeit the wealth and the good social position which awaited him. What excuse could he offer for breaking the engagement? That which he had to bring against Hildur was so inconsequential that it would have turned to air on his lips had he attempted to express it.

But his heart was often heavy, and every time he had an errand down to the parish or the city he bought ale or wine at the shops to drink himself into a good humor.

When he had emptied a couple of bottles, he was again proud of the marriage and pleased with Hildur. Then he didn't understand what it was that pained him.

Gudmund often thought of Helga and longed to meet her. But he fancied that Helga believed him a wretch because he had not kept the promise which he voluntarily made her, but had allowed her to go away. He could neither explain nor excuse himself; therefore, he avoided her.

One morning, when Gudmund was walking up the road, he met Helga, who had been down in the village to buy milk. Gudmund turned about and joined her.

She didn't appear to be pleased with his company and walked rapidly, as if she wished to get away from him, and said nothing. Gudmund, too, kept still because he didn't quite know how he should begin the conversation.

A vehicle was seen on the road, far behind. Gudmund was absorbed in thought and did not mark it, but Helga had seen it and turned abruptly to him: "It is not worth your while to be in my company, Gudmund, for, unless I see wrongly, it is the juryman from Älvåkra and his daughter who come driving back there."

Gudmund glanced up quickly, recognized the horse, and made a movement as if to turn back, but the next instant he straightened up and walked calmly at Helga's side until the vehicle had passed. Then he slackened his pace. Helga continued to walk rapidly, and they parted company without his having said a word to her. But all that day he was better satisfied with himself than he had been in a long while.

V

It was decided that Gudmund and Hildur's wedding should be celebrated at Älvåkra the day following Palm Sunday. On the Friday before, Gudmund drove to town to make some purchases for the homecoming banquet, which was to be held at Närlunda the day after the wedding. In the village he happened across a number of young men from his parish. They knew it was his last trip to the city before the marriage and made it the occasion for a carousal. All insisted that Gudmund must drink, and they succeeded finally in getting him thoroughly intoxicated.

He came home on Saturday morning so late that his father and the men servants had already gone out to their work, and he slept on until late in the afternoon. When he arose and was going to dress himself, he noticed that his coat was torn in several places. "It looks as though I had been in a fight last night," said he, trying to recall what he had been up to. He remembered this much: he had left the public tavern at eleven o'clock in company with his comrades; but where they had gone afterward, he couldn't remember. It was like trying to peer into a great darkness. He did not know if they had only driven around on the streets, or if they had been in somebody's home. He didn't remember whether he or someone else had harnessed the horse, and had no recollection whatever of the drive home.

When he came into the living room of the cottage, it was scoured and arranged for the occasion. All work was over for the day, and members of the household were having coffee. No one spoke of Gudmund's trip. It seemed to be a matter agreed upon that he should have the freedom of living as he chose these last weeks.

Gudmund sat down at the table and had his coffee like the others. As he sat pouring it from the cup into the saucer and back into the cup again to let it cool, Mother Ingeborg, who had finished with hers, took up the newspaper, which had just arrived, and began reading. She read aloud column after column, and Gudmund, his father, and the rest sat and listened.

Among other things which she read, there was an account of a fight that had taken place the night before, on the big square, between a gang of drunken farmers and some laborers. As soon as the police turned up, the fighters fled, but one of them lay dead on the square. The man

44

was carried to the police station, and when no outward injury was found on him, they had tried to resuscitate him. But all attempts had been in vain, and at last they discovered that a knife blade was imbedded in the skull. It was the blade of an uncommonly large clasp-knife that had pierced the brain and was broken off close to the head. The murderer had fled with the knife-handle, but as the police knew perfectly well who had been in the fight, they had hopes of soon finding him.

While Mother Ingeborg was reading this, Gudmund set down the coffee-cup, stuck his hand in his pocket, pulled out a clasp-knife, and glanced at it carelessly. But almost immediately he started, turned the knife over, and poked it into his pocket as quickly as though it had burned him. He did not touch the coffee after that, but sat a long while, perfectly still, with a puzzled expression on his face. His brows were contracted, and it was apparent that he was trying with all his might to think out something.

Finally he stood up, stretched himself, yawned, and walked leisurely toward the door. "I'll have to bestir myself. I haven't been out of doors all day," he said, leaving the room.

About the same time, Erland Erlandsson also arose. He had smoked out his pipe, and now he went into the side room to get some tobacco. As he was standing in there, refilling his pipe, he saw Gudmund walking along. The windows of the side room did not, like those of the main room, face the yard, but looked out upon a little garden plot with a couple of tall apple trees. Beyond the plot lay a bit of swamp land where in the spring of the year there were big pools of water, but which were almost dried out in the summer. Toward this side it was seldom that anyone went. Erland Erlandsson wondered what Gudmund was doing there, and followed him with his eyes. Then he saw that the son stuck his hand into his pocket, drew out some object, and flung it away in the morass. Thereupon he walked back across the little garden plot, leaped a fence, and went down the road.

As soon as his son was out of sight, Erland, in his turn, betook himself, as he should have done, to the swamp. He waded out into the mire, bent down, and picked up something his foot had touched. It was a large clasp-knife with the biggest blade broken off. He turned it over and over and examined it carefully while he still stood in the water. Then he put it into his pocket, but he took it out again and looked at it before returning to the house.

Gudmund did not come home until the household had retired. He went immediately to bed without touching his supper, which was spread in the main room.

Erland Erlandsson and his wife slept in the side room. At daybreak Erland thought he heard footsteps outside the window. He got up, drew aside the curtain, and saw Gudmund walking down to the swamp. He stripped off stockings and shoes and waded out into the water, tramping back and forth, like one who is searching for something. He kept this up for a long while, then he walked back to dry land, as if he intended to go away, but soon turned back to resume his search. A whole hour his father stood watching him. Then Gudmund went back to the house again and to bed.

On Palm Sunday Gudmund was to drive to church. As he started to hitch up the horse, his father came out. "You have forgotten to polish the harness today," he said, as he walked by, for both harness and cart were muddy.

"I have had other things to think of," said Gudmund listlessly, and drove off without doing anything in the matter.

After the service, Gudmund accompanied his betrothed to Älvåkra and remained there all day. A number of young people came to celebrate Hildur's last evening as a maid, and there was dancing till far into the night. Intoxicants were plentiful, but Gudmund did not touch them. The whole evening he had scarcely spoken a word to anyone, but he danced wildly and laughed at times, loudly and

46

stridently, without anyone's knowing what he was so amused over.

Gudmund did not come home until about two in the morning, and when he had stabled the horse he went down to the swamp back of the house. He took off his shoes and stockings, rolled up his trousers, and waded into the water and mud. It was a light spring night, and his father was standing in the side room behind the curtain, watching his son. He saw how he walked bending over the water and searching as on the previous night. He went up on land between times, but after a moment or two he would wade again through the mud. Once he went and fetched a bucket from the barn and began dipping water from the pools, as if he intended to drain them, but really found it unprofitable and set the bucket aside. He tried also with a pole-net. He plowed through the entire swamp-ground with it, but seemed to bring up nothing but mud. He did not go in until the morning was so well on that the people in the house were beginning to bestir themselves. Then he was so tired and spent that he staggered as he walked, and he flung himself upon the bed without undressing.

When the clock struck eight, his father came and wakened him. Gudmund lay upon the bed, his clothing covered with mud and clay, but his father did not ask what he had been doing. He simply said, "It is time now to get up," and closed the door.

After a while Gudmund came downstairs, dressed in his wedding clothes. He was pale, and his eyes wore a troubled expression, but no one had ever seen him look so handsome. His features were as if illumined by an inner light. One felt that one was looking upon something no longer made up of flesh and blood—only of soul and will.

It was solemnly ceremonious down in the main room. His mother was in black, and she had thrown a pretty silk shawl across her shoulders, although she was not to be at the wedding. Fresh birch leaves were arranged in the fire-

47

place. The table was spread, and there was a great quantity of food.

When they had breakfasted, Mother Ingeborg read a hymn and something from the Bible. Then she turned to Gudmund, thanked him for having been a good son, wished him happiness in his new life, and gave him her blessing. Mother Ingeborg could arrange her words well, and Gudmund was deeply moved. The tears welled to his eyes time and again, but he managed to choke them back. His father, too, said a few words. "It will be hard for your parents to lose you," he said, and again Gudmund came near breaking down. All the servants came forward and shook hands with him and thanked him for the past. Tears were in his eyes all the while. He pulled himself together and made several attempts to speak, but could scarcely get a word past his lips.

His father was to accompany him to the wedding and be one of the party. He went out and harnessed the horse, after which he came back and announced that it was time to start. When Gudmund was seated in the cart, he noticed that it was cleansed and burnished. Everything was as bright and shiny as he himself always wished it to be. At the same time he saw, also, how neat everything about the place looked. The driveway had been laid with new gravel; piles of old wood and rubbish, which had lain there all his life, were removed. On each side of the entrance door stood a birch branch, as a gate of honor. A large wreath of blueberry hung on the weathervane, and from every aperture peeped light green birch leaves. Again Gudmund was ready to burst into tears. He grasped his father's hand hard when he was about to start; it was as though he wished to prevent his going.

"Is there something—?" said the father.

"Oh, no!" said Gudmund. "It is best, I dare say, that we go ahead."

Gudmund had to say one more farewell before he was very far from the homestead. It was to Helga from Big

Marsh, who stood waiting at the hedge, where the foliage path leading from her home opened into the highway. The father was driving and stopped when he saw Helga.

"I have been waiting for you, as I wanted to wish you happiness today," said Helga.

Gudmund leaned far out over the cart and shook hands with Helga. He thought that she had grown thin and that her eyelids were red. Very probably she had lain awake and cried all night and was homesick for Närlunda. But now she tried to appear happy and smiled sweetly at him. Again he felt deeply moved but could not speak.

His father, who was reputed never to speak a word until it was called forth by extreme necessity, joined in: "That good wish, I think, Gudmund will be more glad over than any other."

"Yes, of that you may be sure!" said Gudmund. He shook hands with Helga once more, and then they drove on.

Gudmund leaned back in the cart and looked after Helga. When she was hidden from view by a couple of trees, he hastily tore aside the apron of the carriage, as if he wished to jump out.

"Is there anything more you wish to say to Helga?" asked his father.

"No, oh, no!" answered Gudmund and turned round again.

Suddenly Gudmund leaned his head against his father's shoulder and burst out crying.

"What ails you?" asked Erland Erlandsson, drawing in the reins so suddenly that the horse stopped.

"Oh, they are all so good to me and I don't deserve it."

"But you have never done anything wrong, surely?"

"Yes, Father, I have."

"That we can't believe."

"I have killed a human being!"

The father drew a deep breath. It sounded almost like a sigh of relief, and Gudmund raised his head, astonished, and looked at him. His father set the horse in motion again; then he said calmly, "I'm glad you have told of this yourself."

"Did you know it already, Father?"

"I surmised last Saturday evening that there was something wrong. And then I found your knife down in the morass."

"So it was you who found the knife!"

"I found it and I noticed that one of the blades had been broken off."

"Yes, Father, I'm aware that the knife-blade is gone, but still I cannot get it into my head that I did it."

"It was probably done in the drunkenness and delirium."

"I know nothing; I remember nothing. I could see by my clothes that I had been in a fight and I knew that the knife-blade was missing."

"I understand that it was your intention to be silent about this," said the father.

"I thought that perhaps the rest of the party were as irresponsible as myself, and I couldn't remember anything. There was perhaps no other evidence against me than the knife; therefore, I threw it away."

"I comprehend that you must have reasoned in that way."

"You understand, Father, that I do not know who is dead. I had never seen him before, I dare say. I have no recollection of having done it. I didn't think I ought to suffer for what I had not done knowingly. But soon I got to thinking that I must have been mad to throw the knife into the marsh. It dries out in summer, and then anyone might find it. I tried last night and the night before to find it."

"Didn't it occur to you that you should confess?"

"No! Yesterday I thought only of how I could keep it a secret, and I tried to dance and be merry, so that no one would mark any change in me."

"Was it your intention to go to the bridal altar today without confessing? You were assuming a grave responsibility. Didn't you understand that if you were discovered you would drag Hildur and her kin with you into misery?"

"I thought that I was sparing them most by saying nothing."

They drove now as fast as possible. The father seemed to be in haste to arrive, and all the time he talked with his son. He had not said so much to him in all his life before.

"I wonder how you came to think differently?" said he.

"It was because Helga came and wished me luck. Then there was something hard in me that broke. I was touched by something in her. Mother, also, moved me this morning, and I wanted to speak out and tell her that I was not worthy of your love; but then the hardness was still within me and made resistance. But when Helga appeared, it was all over with me. I felt that she really ought to be angry with me who was to blame for her having to leave our home."

"Now I think you are agreed with me that we must let the juryman know this at once," said the father.

"Yes," answered Gudmund in a low tone. "Why, certainly!" he added almost immediately after, louder and firmer. "I don't want to drag Hildur into my misfortune. This she would never forgive me."

"The Älvåkra folk are jealous of their honor, like the rest," remarked the father. "And you may as well know, Gudmund, that when I left home this morning I was thinking that I must tell the juryman your position if you did not decide to do so yourself. I never could have stood silently by and let Hildur marry a man who at any moment might be accused of murder."

He cracked the whip and drove on, faster and faster. "This will be the hardest thing for you," said he, "but we'll try and have it over with quickly. I believe that, to the Juryman's mind, it will be right for you to give yourself up, and they will be kind to you, no doubt."

Gudmund said nothing. His torture increased the

nearer they approached Älvåkra. The father continued talking to keep up his courage.

"I have heard something of this sort before," said he. "There was a bridegroom once who happened to shoot a comrade to death during a hunt. He did not do it intentionally, and it was not discovered that he was the one who had fired the fatal shot. But a day or two later he was to be married, and when he came to the home of the bride, he went to her and said: 'The marriage cannot take place. I do not care to drag you into the misery which awaits me.' But she stood, dressed in bridal wreath and crown, and took him by the hand and led him into the drawing room, where the guests were assembled and all was in readiness for the ceremony. She related in a clear voice what the bridegroom had just said to her. 'I have told of this, that all may know you have practiced no deceit on me.' Then she turned to the bridegroom. 'Now I want to be married to you at once. You are what you are, even though you have met with misfortune, and whatever awaits you, I want to share it equally with you.'"

Just as the father had finished the narrative, they were on the long avenue leading to Älvåkra. Gudmund turned to him with a melancholy smile. "It will not end thus for us," he said.

"Who knows?" said the father, straightening in the cart. He looked upon his son and was again astonished at his beauty this day. "It would not surprise me if something great and unexpected were to come to him," thought he.

There was to have been a church ceremony, and already a crowd of people were gathered at the bride's home to join in the wedding procession. A number of the juryman's relatives from a distance had also arrived. They were sitting on the porch in their best attire, ready for the drive to church. Carts and carriages were strung out in the yard, and one could hear the horses stamping in the stable as they were being curried. The parish fiddler sat on the steps of the storehouse alone, tuning his fiddle.

At a window in the upper story of the cottage stood the bride, dressed and waiting to have a peep at the bridegroom before he had time to discover her.

Erland and Gudmund stepped from the carriage and asked immediately for a private conference with Hildur and her parents. Soon they were all standing in the little room which the juryman used as his study.

"I think you must have read in the papers of that fight in town last Saturday night, where a man was killed," said Gudmund, as rapidly as if he were repeating a lesson.

"Oh, yes, I've read about it, of course," said the juryman.

"I happened to be in town that night," continued Gudmund. Now there was no response. It was as still as death. Gudmund thought they all glared at him with such fury that he was unable to continue. But his father came to his aid.

"Gudmund had been invited out by a few friends. He had probably drunk too much that night, and when he came home he did not know what he had been doing. But it was apparent that he had been in a fight, for his clothes were torn."

Gudmund saw that the dread which the others felt increased with every word that was said, but he himself was growing calmer. There awoke in him a sense of defiance, and he took up the words again: "When the paper came on Saturday evening and I read of the fight and of the knife-blade which was imbedded in the man's skull, I took out my knife and saw that a blade was missing."

"It is bad news that Gudmund brings with him," said the juryman. "It would have been better had he told us of this yesterday."

Gudmund was silent, and now his father came to the rescue again. "It was not so easy for Gudmund. It was a great temptation to keep quiet about the whole affair. He is losing much by this confession."

"We may be glad that he has spoken now, and that we

have not been tricked and dragged into this wretched affair," said the juryman bitterly.

Gudmund kept his eyes fixed on Hildur all the while. She was adorned with veil and crown, and now he saw how she raised her hand and drew out one of the large pins which held the crown in place. She seemed to do this unconsciously. When she observed that Gudmund's glance rested upon her, she stuck the pin in again.

"It is not yet fully proved that Gudmund is the slayer," said his father, "but I can well understand that you wish the wedding postponed until everything has been cleared up."

"It is not worth while to talk of postponement," said the juryman. "I think that Gudmund's case is clear enough for us to decide that all is over between him and Hildur now."

Gudmund did not at once reply to this judgment. He walked over to his betrothed and put out his hand. She sat perfectly still and seemed not to see him. "Won't you say farewell to me, Hildur?"

Then she looked up, and her large eyes stared coldly at him. "Was it with that hand you guided the knife?" she asked.

Gudmund did not answer her, but turned to the juryman. "Now I am sure of my case," he said. "It is useless to talk of a wedding."

With this the conference was ended, and Gudmund and Erland went their way.

They had to pass through a number of rooms and corridors before they came out, and everywhere they saw preparations for the wedding. The door leading to the kitchen was open, and they saw many bustling about in eager haste. The smell of roasts and of baking penetrated the air; the whole fireplace was covered with large and small pots and pans, and the copper saucepans, which usually decorated the walls, were down and in use. "Fancy, it is for my wedding that they are puttering like this!" thought Gudmund as he was passing.

He caught a glimpse, so to speak, of all the wealth of this old peasant estate as he wandered through the house. He saw the dining hall, where the long tables were set with a long row of silver goblets and decanters. He passed by the clothes-press, where the floor was covered with great chests and where the walls were hung with an end-less array of wearing apparel. When he came out in the yard, he saw many vehicles, old and new, and fine horses being led out from the stable, and gorgeous carriage robes placed in the carriages. He looked out across a couple of farms with cow-sheds, barns, sheep-folds, storehouses, sheds, larders, and many other buildings. "All this might have been mine," he thought as he seated himself in the cart.

Suddenly he was seized with a sense of bitter regret. He would have liked to throw himself out of the cart and go in and say that what he had told them was not true. He had only wished to joke with them and frighten them. It was awfully stupid of him to confess. Of what use had it been to him to confess? The dead was dead. No, this con-fession carried nothing with it save his ruin.

These last weeks he had not been very enthusiastic over this marriage. But now, when he must renounce it, he realized what it was worth to him. It meant much to lose Hildur Ericsdotter and all that went with her. What did it matter that she was domineering and opinionated? She was still the peer of all in these regions, and through her he would have come by great power and honor.

It was not only Hildur and her possessions he was missing, but minor things as well. At this moment he should have been driving to the church, and all who looked upon him would have envied him. And it was today that he should have sat at the head of the wedding table and been in the thick of the dancing and the gaiety. It was his great luck-day that was going from him.

Erland turned time and again to his son and looked at him. Now he was not so handsome or transfigured as he had been in the morning, but sat there listless and heavy and dull-eyed. The father wondered if the son regretted having confessed and meant to question him about it, but thought it best to be silent.

"Where are we driving to now?" asked Gudmund presently. "Wouldn't it be as well to go at once to the sheriff?"

"You had better go home first and have a good sleep," said the father. "You have not had much sleep these last nights, I dare say."

"Mother will be frightened when she sees us."

"She won't be surprised," answered the father, "for she knows quite as much as I do. She will be glad, of course, that you have confessed."

"I believe Mother and the rest of you at home are glad to get me into prison," snarled Gudmund.

"We know that you are losing a good deal in acting rightly," said the father. "We can't help but be glad because you have conquered yourself."

Gudmund felt that he could not endure going home and having to listen to all who would commend him because he had spoiled his future. He sought some excuse that he might escape meeting anyone until he had recovered his poise. Then they drove by the place where the path led to Big Marsh. "Will you stop here, Father? I think I'll run up to see Helga and have a talk with her."

Willingly the father reined in the horse. "Only come home as quickly as you can, that you may rest yourself," said he.

Gudmund went into the woods and was soon out of sight. He did not think of seeking Helga; he was only thinking of being alone, so that he wouldn't have to control himself. He felt an unreasonable anger toward everything—kicked at stones that lay in his path, and paused sometimes to break off a big branch only because a leaf had brushed his cheek.

He followed the path to Big Marsh, but walked past the

56

croft and up the hill which lay above it. He had wandered off the path, and in order to reach the hilltop he must cross a broad ridge of sharp, jagged rocks. It was a hazardous tramp over the sharp rock edges. He might have broken both arms and legs had he made a misstep. He understood this perfectly, but went on as if it amused him to run into danger. "If I were to fall and hurt myself, no one can find me up here," thought he. "What of it? I may as well die here as to sit for years within prison walls."

All went well, however, and a few moments later he was up on High Peak. Once a forest fire had swept the mountain. The highest point was still bare, and from there one had a seven-mile outlook. He saw valleys and lakes, dark forest tracts and flourishing towns, churches and manors, little woodland crofts and large villages. Far in the distance lay the city, enveloped in a white haze from which a pair of gleaming spires peeped out. Public roads wound through the valleys, and a railway train was rushing along the border of the forest. It was a whole kingdom that he saw.

He flung himself upon the ground, all the while keeping his eyes riveted upon the vast outlook. There was something grand and majestic about the landscape before him, which made him feel himself and his sorrows small and insignificant.

He remembered how, when a child, he had read that the tempter led Jesus up to a high mountain and showed him all the world's glories, and he always fancied that they had stood up here on Great Peak, and he repeated the old words: "All these things will I give thee if thou wilt fall down and worship me."

All of a sudden he was thinking that a similar temptation had come to him these last days. Certainly the tempter had not borne him to a high mountain and shown him all the glories and powers of this world! "Only be silent about the evil which you think you have done," said he, "and I will give you all these things."

As Gudmund thought on this, a grain of satisfaction came to him. "I have answered no," he said, and suddenly he understood what it had meant for him. If he had kept silent, would he not have been compelled to worship the tempter all his life? He would have been a timid and faint-hearted man; simply a slave to his possessions. The fear of discovery would always have weighed upon him. Nevermore would he have felt himself a free man.

A great peace came over Gudmund. He was happy in the consciousness that he had done right. When he thought back to the past days, he felt that he had groped his way out of a great darkness. It was wonderful that he had come out right finally. He asked himself how he had ever happened to go astray. "It was because they were so kind to me at home," he thought, "and the best help was that Helga came and wished me happiness."

He lay up there on the mountain a little longer, but presently he felt that he must go home to his father and mother and tell them that he was at peace with himself. When he rose to go, he saw Helga sitting on a ledge a little farther down the mountain.

Where she sat, she had not the big, broad outlook which he enjoyed; only a little glint of the valley was visible to her. This was in the direction where Närlunda lay, and possibly she could see a portion of the farm. When Gudmund discovered her, he felt that his heart, which all the day before had labored heavily and anxiously, began to beat lightly and merrily; at the same time such a thrill of joy ran through him that he stood still and marveled at himself. "What has come over me? What is this?" he wondered, as the blood surged through his body and happiness gripped him with a force that was almost painful. At last he said to himself in a surprised tone: "Why, it is she that I'm fond of! Think, that I did not know it until now!"

It took hold of him with the strength of a loosened torrent. He had been bound the whole time he knew her. All that had drawn him to her he had held back. Now, at last, he was freed from the thought of marrying someone else—free to love her.

"Helga!" he cried, rushing down the steep to her. She turned round with a terrified shriek. "Don't be frightened! It is only I."

"But are you not at church being married?"

"No, indeed! There will be no wedding today. She does not want me—she—Hildur."

Helga rose. She placed her hand on her heart and closed her eyes. At that moment she must have thought it was not Gudmund who had come. It must be that her eyes and ears were bewitched in the forest. Yet it was sweet and dear of him to come, if only in a vision! She closed her eyes and stood motionless to keep this vision a few seconds longer.

Gudmund was wild and dizzy from the great love that had flamed up in him. As soon as he came down to Helga, he threw his arms around her and kissed her, and she let it happen, for she was absolutely stupefied with surprise. It was too wonderful to believe that he, who should now be standing in church beside his bride, actually could have come here to the forest. This phantom or ghost of him that had come to her may as well kiss her.

But while Gudmund was kissing Helga, she awoke and pushed him from her. She began to shower him with questions. Was it really he? What was he doing in the forest? Had any misfortune happened to him? Why was the wedding postponed? Was Hildur ill? Did the clergyman have a stroke in church?

Gudmund had not wished to talk to her of anything in the world save his love, but she forced him to tell her what had occurred. While he was speaking she sat still and listened with rapt attention.

She did not interrupt him until he mentioned the broken blade. Then she leaped up suddenly and asked if it was his clasp-knife, the one he had when she served with them.

59

"Yes, it was just that one," said he.

"How many blades were broken off?" she asked.

"Only one," he answered.

Then Helga's head began working. She sat with knit brows trying to recall something. Wait! Why, certainly she remembered distinctly that she had borrowed the knife from him to shave wood with the day before she left. She had broken it then, but she had never told him of it. He had avoided her, and at that time he had not wished to hold any converse with her. And, of course, the knife had been in his pocket ever since and he hadn't noticed that it was broken.

She raised her head and was about to tell him of this, but he went on talking of his visit that morning to the house where the wedding was to have been celebrated, and she wanted to let him finish. When she heard how he had parted from Hildur, she thought it such a terrible misfortune that she began upbraiding him. "This is your own fault," said she. "You and your father came and frightened the life out of her with the shocking news. She would not have answered thus had she been mistress of herself. I want to say to you that I believe she regrets it at this very moment."

"Let her regret it as much as she likes, for all of me!" said Gudmund. "I know now that she is the sort who thinks only of herself. I am glad I'm rid of her!"

Helga pressed her lips, as if to keep the great secret from escaping. There was much for her to think about. It was more than a question of clearing Gudmund of the murder; the wretched affair had also dragged with it enmity between Gudmund and his sweetheart. Perhaps she might try to adjust this matter with the help of what she knew.

Again she sat silent and pondered until Gudmund began telling that he had transferred his affections to her.

But to her this seemed to be the greatest misfortune he had met with that day. It was bad that he was about to miss the advantageous marriage, but still worse were he to woo a girl like herself. "No, such things you must not say to me," she said, rising abruptly.

"Why shouldn't I say this to you?" asked Gudmund, turning pale. "Perhaps it is with you as with Hildur—you are afraid of me?"

"No, that's not the reason."

She wanted to explain how he was seeking his own ruin, but he was not listening to her. "I have heard said that there were women-folk in olden times who stood side by side with men when they were in trouble; but that kind one does not encounter nowadays."

A tremor passed through Helga. She could have thrown her arms around his neck, but remained perfectly still. Today it was she who must be sensible.

"True, I should not have asked you to become my wife on the day that I must go to prison. You see, if I only knew that you would wait for me until I'm free again, I should go through all the hardship with courage. Everyone will now regard me as a criminal, as one who drinks and murders. If only there were someone who could think of me with affection!—this would sustain me more than anything else."

"You know, surely, that I shall never think anything but good of you, Gudmund."

Helga was so still! Gudmund's entreaties were becoming almost too much for her. She didn't know how she should escape him. He apprehended nothing of this, but began thinking he had been mistaken. She could not feel toward him as he did toward her. He came very close and looked at her, as though he wanted to look through her. "Are you not sitting on this particular ledge of the mountain that you may look down to Närlunda?"

"Yes."

"Don't you long night and day to be there?"

"Yes, but I'm not longing for any person."

"And you don't care for me?"

61

"Yes, but I don't want to marry you."

"Whom do you care for, then?"

Helga was silent.

"Is it Per Mårtensson?"

"I have already told you that I liked him," she said, exhausted by the strain of it all.

Gudmund stood for a moment, with tense features, and looked at her. "Farewell then! Now we must go our separate ways, you and I," said he. With that he made a long jump from this ledge of the mountain down to the next landing and disappeared among the trees.

VI

Gudmund was hardly out of sight when Helga rushed down the mountain in another direction. She ran past the marsh without stopping and hurried over the wooded hills as fast as she could and down the road. She stopped at the first farmhouse she came to and asked for the loan of a horse and car to drive to Älvåkra. She said that it was a matter of life and death and promised to pay for the help. The church folk had already returned to their homes and were talking of the adjourned wedding. They were all very much excited and very solicitous and were eager to help Helga, since she appeared to have an important errand to the home of the bride.

At Älvåkra, Hildur Ericsdotter sat in a little room on the upper floor where she had dressed as a bride. Her mother and several other peasant women were with her. Hildur did not weep; she was unusually quiet, and so pale that she looked as though she might be ill at any moment. The women talked all the while of Gudmund. All blamed him and seemed to regard it as a fortunate thing that she was rid of him. Some thought that Gudmund had shown very little consideration for his parents-in-law in not letting them know on Palm Sunday how matters stood with him. Others, again, said that one who had had such happiness awaiting him should have known how to take better care of himself. A few congratulated Hildur because she had escaped marrying a man who could drink himself so full that he did not know what he was doing.

Amid this, Hildur was losing her patience and rose to go out. As soon as she was outside the door, her best friend, a young peasant girl, came and whispered something to her. "There is someone below who wants to speak with you."

"Is it Gudmund?" asked Hildur, and a spark of life came into her eyes.

"No, but it may be a messenger from him. She would not divulge the nature of her errand to anyone but yourself, she declared."

Hildur had been sitting thinking all day that someone must come who could put an end to her misery. She could not comprehend that such a dreadful misfortune should come to her. She felt that something ought to happen that she might again don her crown and wreath, so they could proceed with the wedding. When she heard now of a messenger from Gudmund, she was interested and immediately went out to the kitchen hall and looked for her.

Hildur probably wondered why Gudmund had sent Helga to her, but she thought that perhaps he couldn't find any other messenger on a holiday, and greeted her pleasantly. She motioned to Helga to come with her into the dairy across the yard. "I know no other place where we can be alone," she said. "The house is still full of guests."

As soon as they were inside, Helga went close up to Hildur and looked her square in the face. "Before I say anything more, I must know if you love Gudmund."

Hildur winced. It was painful for her to be obliged to exchange a single word with Helga, and she had no desire to make a confidant of her. But now it was a case of necessity, and she forced herself to answer, "Why else do you suppose I wished to marry him?"

"I mean, do you still love him?"

Hildur was like stone, but she could not lie under the other woman's searching glance. "Perhaps I have never loved him so much as today," she said, but she said this so feebly that one might think it hurt her to speak out.

"Then come with me at once!" said Helga. "I have a wagon down the road. Go in after a cloak or something to wrap around you; then we'll drive to Närlunda."

"What good would it do for me to go there?" asked Hildur.

"You must go there and say you want to be Gudmund's, no matter what he may have done, and that you will wait faithfully for him while he is in prison."

"Why should I say this?"

"So all will be well between you."

"But that is impossible. I don't want to marry anyone who has been in prison!"

Helga staggered back, as though she had bumped against a wall, but she quickly regained her courage. She could understand that one who was rich and powerful, like Hildur, must think thus. "I should not come and ask you to go to Närlunda did I not know that Gudmund was innocent," said she.

Now it was Hildur who came a step or two toward Helga. "Do you know this for certain, or is it only something which you imagine?"

"It will be better for us to get into the cart immediately; then I can talk on the way."

"No, you must first explain what you mean; I must know what I'm doing."

Helga was in such a fever of excitement that she could hardly stand still; nevertheless she had to make up her mind to tell Hildur how she happened to know that Gudmund was not the murderer.

"Didn't you tell Gudmund of this at once?"

"No, I'm telling it now to Hildur. No one else knows of it."

"And why do you come to me with this?"

"That all may be well between you two. He will soon learn that he has done no wrong; but I want you to go to him as if of your own accord, and make it up."

"Shan't I say that I know he is innocent?"

"You must come entirely of your own accord and must never let him know I have spoken to you; otherwise he will never forgive you for what you said to him this morning."

Hildur listened quietly. There was something in this which she had never met with in her life before, and she was striving to make it clear to herself. "Do you know that it was I who wanted you to leave Närlunda?"

"I know, of course, that it was not the folk at Närlunda who wished me away."

"I can't comprehend that you should come to me today with the desire to help me."

"Only come along now, Hildur, so all will be well!"

Hildur stared at Helga, trying all the while to reason it out. "Perhaps Gudmund loves you?" she blurted out.

And now Helga's patience was exhausted. "What could I be to him?" she said sharply. "You know, Hildur, that I am only a poor croft girl, and that's not the worst about me!"

The two young women stole unobserved from the homestead and were soon seated in the cart. Helga held the reins, and she did not spare the horse, but drove at full speed. Both girls were silent. Hildur sat gazing at Helga. She marveled at her and was thinking more of her than of anything else.

As they were nearing the Erlandsson farm, Helga gave the reins to Hildur. "Now you must go alone to the house and talk with Gudmund. I'll follow a little later and tell him about the knife. But you mustn't say a word to Gudmund about my having brought you here."

Gudmund sat in the living room at Närlunda beside his mother and talked with her. His father was sitting a little way from them, smoking. He looked pleased and said not a word. It was apparent that he thought everything was going now as it should and that it was not necessary for him to interfere.

"I wonder, Mother, what you would have said if you had got Helga for a daughter-in-law?" ventured Gudmund.

Mother Ingeborg raised her head and said in a firm voice, "I will with pleasure welcome any daughter-in-law if I only know that she loves you as a wife should love her husband."

This was barely spoken when they saw Hildur Ericsdotter drive into the yard. She came immediately into the cottage and was unlike herself in many respects. She did not step into the room with her usual briskness, but it appeared almost as though she were inclined to pause near the door, like some poor beggarwoman.

However, she came forward finally and shook hands with Mother Ingeborg and Erland. Then she turned to Gudmund: "It is with you that I would have a word or two."

Gudmund arose, and they went into the side room. He arranged a chair for Hildur, but she did not seat herself. She blushed with embarrassment, and the words dropped slowly and heavily from her lips. "I was—yes, it was much too hard—that which I said to you this morning."

"We came so abruptly, Hildur," said Gudmund.

She grew still more red and embarrassed. I should have thought twice. We could—it would of course—"

"It is probably best as it is, Hildur. It is nothing to speak of now, but it was kind of you to come."

She put her hands to her face, drew a breath as deep as a sigh, then raised her head again.

"No!" she said, "I can't do it in this way. I don't want you to think that I'm better than I am. There was some-one who came to me and told me that you were not guilty and advised me to hurry over here at once and make everything right again. And I was not to mention that I already knew you were innocent, for then you wouldn't

66

think it so noble of me to come. Now I want to say to you that I wish I had thought of this myself, but I hadn't. But I have longed for you all day and wished that all might be well between us. Whichever way it turns out, I want to say that I am glad you are innocent."

"Who advised you to do this?" asked Gudmund.

"I was not to tell you that."

"I am surprised that anyone should know of it. Father has but just returned from the sheriff. He telegraphed to the city, and an answer has come that the real murderer has already been found."

As Gudmund was relating this, Hildur felt that her legs were beginning to shake, and she sat down quickly in the chair. She was frightened because Gudmund was so calm and pleasant, and she was beginning to perceive that he was wholly out of her power. "I can understand that you can never forget how I behaved to you this forenoon."

"Surely I can forgive you that," he said in the same even tone. "We will never speak of the matter again."

She shivered, dropped her eyes, and sat as though she were expecting something. "It was simply a stroke of good fortune, Hildur," he said, coming forward and grasping her hand, "that it is over between us, for today it became clear to me that I love another. I think I have been fond of her for a long time, but I did not know it until today."

"Whom do you care for, Gudmund?" came in a colorless voice from Hildur.

"It doesn't matter. I shall not marry her, as she does not care for me, nor can I marry anyone else."

Hildur raised her head. It was not easy to tell what was taking place in her. At this moment she felt that she, the rich farmer's daughter, with all her beauty and all her possessions, was nothing to Gudmund. She was proud and did not wish to part from him without teaching him that she had a value of her own, apart from all the external things. "I want you to tell me, Gudmund, if it is Helga from Big Marsh whom you love."

67

Gudmund was silent.

"It was she who came to me and taught me what I should do that all might be well between us. She knew you were innocent, but she did not say so to you. She let me know it first."

Gudmund looked her steadily in the eyes. "Do you think this means that she has a great affection for me?"

"You may be sure of it, Gudmund. I can prove it. No one in the world could love you more than she does."

He walked rapidly across the floor and back, then he stopped suddenly before Hildur. "And you—why do you tell me this?"

"Surely I do not wish to stand beneath Helga in magnanimity!"

"Oh, Hildur, Hildur!" he cried, placing his hands on her shoulders and shaking her to give vent to his emotion. "You don't know, oh, you don't know how much I like you at this moment! You don't know how happy you have made me!"

Helga sat by the roadside and waited. With her cheek resting on her hand, she sat and pictured Hildur and Gudmund together and thought how happy they must be now.

While she sat thus, a servant from Närlunda came along. He stopped when he saw her. "I suppose you have heard of that affair which concerns Gudmund?"

She had.

"It was not true, fortunately. The real murderer is already in custody."

"I knew it couldn't be true," said Helga. Thereupon the man went, and Helga sat there alone, as before. So they knew it already down there! It was not necessary for her to go to Närlunda and tell of it.

She felt herself so strangely shut out! Earlier in the day she had been so eager. She had not thought of herself—only that Gudmund and Hildur's marriage should take place. But now it flashed upon her how alone she

68

was. And it was hard not to be something to those of whom one is fond. Gudmund did not need her now, and her own child had been appropriated by her mother, who would hardly allow her to look at it.

She was thinking that she had better rise and go home, but the hills appeared long and difficult to her. She didn't know how she should ever be able to climb them.

A vehicle came along from the direction of Närlunda. Hildur and Gudmund were seated in the cart. Now they were probably on their way to Älvåkra to tell that they were reconciled. Tomorrow the wedding would take place.

When they discovered Helga, they stopped the horse. Gudmund handed the reins to Hildur and jumped down. Hildur nodded to Helga and drove on.

Gudmund remained standing on the road and facing Helga. "I am glad you are sitting here, Helga," he said. "I thought that I would have to go up to Big Marsh to meet you."

He said this abruptly, almost harshly; at the same time, he gripped her hand tightly. And she read in his eyes that he knew now where he had her. Now she could no more escape from him.

The Airship

Father and the boys are seated one rainy October evening in a third-class railway coach on their way to Stockholm. The father is sitting by himself on one bench, and the boys sit close together directly opposite him, reading a Jules Verne romance entitled *Six Weeks in a Balloon*. The book is much worn. The boys know it almost by heart and have held endless discussions on it, but they always read it with the same pleasure. They have forgotten everything else to follow the daring sailors of the air all over Africa, and seldom raise their eyes from the book to glance at the Swedish towns they are traveling through.

The boys are very like each other. They are the same height, are dressed alike, with blue caps and gray overcoats, and both have large dreamy eyes and little pug noses. They are always good friends, always together, do not bother with other children, and are forever talking about inventions and exploring expeditions. In point of talent they are quite unlike. Lennart, the elder, who is thirteen, is backward in his studies at the High School and can hardly keep up with his class in any theme. To make up for this, he is very handy and enterprising. He is going to be an inventor and works all the time on a flying-machine which he is constructing. Hugo is a year younger than Lennart, but he is quicker at study and is already in the same grade as his brother. He doesn't find studying any special fun, either; but, on the other hand, he is a great sportsman—a ski-runner, a cyclist, and a skater. He intends to start out on voyages of discovery when he is grown up. As soon as Lennart's airship is ready, Hugo is going to travel in it in order to explore what is still left of this globe to be discovered.

Their father is a tall, thin man with a sunken chest, a

haggard face, and pretty, slender hands. He is carelessly dressed. His shirt bosom is wrinkled and the coat band pokes up at the neck; his vest is buttoned wrongly and his socks sag down over his shoes. He wears his hair so long at the neck that it hangs on his coat collar. This is due, not to carelessness, but to habit and taste.

The father is a descendant of an old musical family from far back in a rural district, and he has brought with him into the world two strong inclinations, one of which is a great musical talent; it was this that first came to light. He was graduated from the Academy in Stockholm and then studied a few years abroad, and during these study years made such brilliant progress that both he and his teacher thought he would someday be a great and world-renowned violinist. He certainly had talent enough to reach the goal, but he lacked grit and perseverance. He couldn't fight his way to any sort of standing out in the world, but soon came home again and accepted a situation as organist in a country town. At the start, he felt ashamed because he had not lived up to the expectations of everyone, but he felt, also, that it was good to have an assured income and not be forced to depend any longer upon the charity of others.

Shortly after he had got the appointment, he married, and a few years later he was perfectly satisfied with his lot. He had a pretty little home, a cheerful and contented wife, and two little boys. He was the town favorite, fêted, and in great demand everywhere. But then there came a time when all this did not seem to satisfy him. He longed to go out in the world once more and try his luck, but he felt bound at home because he had a wife and children.

More than all, it was the wife who had persuaded him to give up this journey. She had not believed that he would succeed any better now than before. She felt they were so happy that there was no need for him to strive after anything else. Unquestionably she made a mistake in this instance, but she also lived to regret it bitterly, for, from

71

that time on, the other family trait showed itself. When his yearning for success and fame was not satisfied, he tried to console himself with drinking.

Now it turned out with him, as was usual with folk of his family, that he drank inordinately. By degrees he became an entirely different person. He was no longer charming or lovable, but harsh and cruel, and the greatest misfortune of all was that he conceived a terrible hatred for his wife and tortured her in every conceivable way, both when he was drunk and when he wasn't.

So the boys did not have a good home, and their childhood would have been very unhappy were they not able to create for themselves a little world of their own, filled with machine models, exploring schemes, and books of adventure. The only one who ever caught a glimpse of this world is the mother. The father hasn't even a suspicion of its existence, nor can he talk with the boys about anything that interests them. He disturbs them, time and again, by asking if they don't think it will be fun to see Stockholm; if they are not glad to be out traveling with father, and other things in that way, to which the boys give brief replies, in order that they may immediately bury themselves in the book again. Nevertheless the father continues to question the boys. He thinks they are charmed with his affability, although they are too bashful to show it.

"They have been too long under petticoat rule," he thinks. "They have become timid and namby-pamby. There will be some go in them now, when I take them in hand." Father is mistaken. It is not because the boys are bashful that they answer him so briefly; it simply shows that they are well brought up and do not wish to hurt his feelings. If they were not polite, they would answer him in a very different manner. "Why should we think it fun to be traveling with father?" they would then say. "Father must think himself something wonderful, but we know, of course, that he is only a poor wreck of a man. And why should we be glad to see Stockholm? We understand very well that it is not for our sakes that Father has taken us along, but only to make Mother unhappy!"

It would be wiser, no doubt, if the father were to let the boys read without interrupting them. They are sad and apprehensive, and it irritates them to see him in a good humor. "It is only because he knows that mother is sitting at home crying that he is so happy today," they whisper to each other.

Father's questions finally bring matters to this pass: the boys read no more, although they continue to sit bent over the book. Instead, their thoughts begin in bitterness to embrace all that they have had to endure on their father's account. They remember the time when he drank himself full in the morning and came staggering up the street, with a crowd of school boys after him—poking fun at him. They recall how the other boys teased them and gave them nicknames because they had a father who drank. They have been put to shame for their father. They have been forced to live in a state of constant anxiety for his sake, and as soon as they are having any enjoyment, he always comes and spoils their fun. It is no small register of sins that they are setting down against him! The boys are very meek and patient, but they feel a greater and greater wrath springing up in them.

He should at least understand that, as yet, they cannot forgive him for the great wrong he did them yesterday. This was by far the worst wrong he had ever done them.

It seems that, last year, Mother and the boys decided to part from Father. For a number of years, he had been persecuting and torturing her in every possible way, but she was loath to part from him and remained, so that he wouldn't go altogether to rack and ruin. But now, at last, she wanted to do it for the sake of her boys. She had noticed that their father made them unhappy, and realized that she must take them away from this misery and provide them with a good and peaceable home.

When the spring school term was over, she sent them

to her parents in the country, and she herself went abroad in order to obtain a divorce in the easiest way possible. She regretted that, by going about it in this way, it would appear as though it were her fault that the marriage was dissolved; but that she must submit to. She was even less pleased when the courts turned the boys over to the father because she was a runaway wife. She consoled herself with the thought that he couldn't possibly wish to keep the children, but she had felt quite ill at ease.

As soon as the divorce was settled, she came back and took a small apartment where she and the boys were to live. In two days she had everything in readiness, so that they could come home to her.

It was the happiest day the boys had experienced. The entire apartment consisted of one large living room and a big kitchen, but everything was new and pretty, and Mother had arranged the place so cozily. The big room she and they were to use daytimes as a workroom, and nights they were to sleep there. The kitchen was light and comfortable. There they would eat, and in a little closet off the kitchen Mother had her bed.

She had told them that they would be very poor. She had secured a place as singing teacher at the girls' school, and this was all they had to live on. They couldn't afford to keep a servant, but must get along all by themselves. The boys were in ecstasies over everything—most of all, because they might help along. They volunteered to carry water and wood. They were to brush their own shoes and make their own beds. It was their only fun to think up all that they were going to do!

There was a little wardrobe in which Lennart was to keep all his mechanical apparatus. He was to have the key himself, and no one but Hugo and he should go in there.

But the boys were allowed to be happy with their mother only for a single day. Afterward their father spoiled their pleasure, as he had always done as far back as they could remember. Mother told them she had heard that their father had received a legacy of a few thousand kronor, and that he had resigned from his position as organist and was going to move to Stockholm. Both they and Mother were glad that he was leaving town, so they would escape meeting him on the streets. And then a friend of Father's had called on mother to tell her that Father wanted to take the boys with him to Stockholm.

Mother had wept and begged that she might keep her boys, but Father's messenger had answered her that her husband was determined to have the boys under his guardianship. If they did not come willingly, he would let the police fetch them. He bade Mother read through the divorce papers, and there it said plainly that the boys would belong to their father. This, of course, she already knew. It was not to be gainsaid.

Father's friend had said many nice things of Father and had told her of how much he loved his sons, and for this reason he wanted them to be with him. But the boys knew that Father was taking them away solely for the purpose of torturing Mother. She would have to live in a state of continual anxiety for them. The whole thing was nothing but malice and revenge!

But Father had his own way, and here they were now, on their way to Stockholm. And right opposite them their father sits, rejoicing in the thought that he has made their mother unhappy. With every second that passes, the thought of having to live with Father becomes more repellent. Are they then wholly in his power? Will there be no help for this?

Father leans back in his seat, and after a bit he falls asleep. Immediately the boys begin whispering to each other very earnestly. It isn't difficult for them to come to a decision. The whole day they have been sitting there thinking that they ought to run away. They conclude to steal out onto the platform and to jump from the train when it goes through a big forest. Then they will build themselves a hut in the most secluded spot in the forest, and live all by themselves and never show themselves to a human being.

While the boys are laying their plans, the train stops at a station, and a peasant woman, leading a little boy by the hand, comes into the coupé. She is dressed in black, with a shawl on her head, and has a kind and friendly appearance. She removes the little one's overcoat, which is wet from the rain, and wraps a shawl around him. Then she takes off his shoes and stockings, dries his little cold feet, takes dry shoes and stockings from a bundle, and puts them on him. Then she gives him a stick of candy and lays him down on the seat with his head resting on her lap, that he might sleep.

First one boy, then the other casts a glance over at the peasant woman. These glances become more frequent, and suddenly the eyes of both boys fill with tears. Then they look up no more, but keep their eyes obstinately lowered.

It seems that when the peasant woman entered someone else—someone who was invisible and imperceptible to all, save the boys—came into the coupé. The boys fancied that she came and sat down between them and took their hands in hers, as she had done late last night when it was settled that they must leave her, and she was talking to them now as she did then. "You must promise me that you will not be angry with Father for my sake. Father has never been able to forgive me for preventing him from going abroad. He thinks it is my fault that he has never amounted to anything and that he drinks. He can never punish me enough. But you mustn't be angry at him on that account. Now, when you are to live with Father, you must promise me that you will be kind to him. You must not quarrel with him and you are to look after his needs as well as you can. This you must promise me, otherwise I don't know how I can ever let you go." And the boys promised. "You mustn't run away from Father, promise me that!" Mother had said. That they had also promised.

The boys are as good as their word, and the instant

76

they happen to think that they had given Mother these promises, they abandon all thought of flight. Father sleeps all the while and they remain patiently in their places. Then they resume their reading with redoubled zeal, and their friend, the good Jules Verne, soon takes them away from many heavy sorrows to Africa's happy wonder world.

Far out on the south side of the city, father has rented two rooms and a kitchen on the ground floor, with an entrance from the court and an outlook over a narrow yard. The apartment has long been in use; it has gone from family to family, without ever having been renovated. The wall paper is full of tears and spots; the ceilings are sooty; a couple of windowpanes are cracked, and the kitchen floor is so worn that it is full of ruts. Expressmen have brought the furniture cases from the railway station and left them there—helter skelter. Father and the boys are now unpacking. Father stands with ax raised to hack open a box. The boys are taking out glass and porcelain ware from another box, and are arranging them in a wall cupboard. They are handy and work eagerly, but the father never stops cautioning them to be careful, and forbids their carrying more than one glass or plate at a time. Meanwhile it goes slowly with Father's own work. His hands are fumbly and powerless, and he works himself into a sweat without getting the lock off the box. He lays down the ax, walks around the box, and wonders if it's the bottom that is uppermost. Then one of the boys takes hold of the ax and begins to bend the lock, but Father pushes him aside. "That lock is nailed down too hard. Surely you don't imagine that you can force the lock when Father couldn't do it? Only a regular workman can open that box," says Father, putting on his hat and coat to go and fetch the janitor.

Father is hardly outside the door when an idea strikes him. Instantly he understands why he has no strength in his hands. It is still quite early in the morning and he has not consumed anything which could set the blood in motion. If he were to step into a café and have a cognac, he would get back his strength and could manage without help. This is better than calling the janitor.

Then Father goes into the street to try and hunt up a café. When he returns to the little apartment on the court, it is eight o'clock in the evening.

In Father's youth, when he attended the Academy, he had lived at the south end of the city. He was then a member of a double quartet, mostly made up of choristers and petty tradesmen, who used to meet in a cellar near Mosebacke. Father had taken a notion to go and see if the little cellar was still there. It was, in fact, and Father had the luck to run across a pair of old comrades who were seated there having their breakfast. They had received him with the greatest delight, had invited him to breakfast, and had celebrated his advent in Stockholm in the friendliest way possible. When the breakfast was over, finally, Father wanted to go home and unpack his furniture, but his friends persuaded him to remain and take dinner with them. This function was so long drawn out that he hadn't been able to go home until around eight o'clock. And it had cost him more than a slight effort to tear himself away from the lively place that early.

When Father comes home, the boys are in the dark, for they have no matches. Father has a match in his pocket, and when he has lighted a little stump of a candle, which luckily had come along with their furnishings, he sees that the boys are hot and dusty, but well and happy and apparently very well-pleased with their day.

In the rooms, the furniture is arranged alongside the walls, the boxes have been removed and straw and papers have been swept away. Hugo is just turning down the boys' beds in the outer room. The inner room is to be Father's bedroom, and there stands his bed, turned down with as great care as he could possibly wish.

Now a sudden revulsion of feeling possesses him. When he came home, he was displeased with himself

78

because he had gone away from his work and had left the boys without food, but now, when he sees that they are in good spirits and not in any distress, he regrets that, for their sakes, he should have left his friends; and he becomes irritable and quarrelsome.

He sees, no doubt, that the boys are proud of all the work they have accomplished and expect him to praise them, but this he is not at all inclined to do. Instead, he asks who has been here and helped them, and begs them to remember that here in Stockholm one gets nothing without money, and that the janitor must be paid for all he does. The boys answer that they have had no assistance and have got on by themselves. But father continues to grumble. It was wrong of them to open the big box. They might have hurt themselves on it. Had he not forbidden them to open it? Now they would have to obey him. He is the one who must answer for their welfare.

He takes the candle, goes out into the kitchen, and peeps into the cupboards. The scanty supply of glass and porcelain is arranged on the shelves in an orderly manner. He scrutinizes everything very carefully to find an excuse for further complaint.

All of a sudden he catches sight of some leavings from the boys' supper, and begins immediately to grumble because they have had chicken. Where did they get it from? Do they think of living like princes? Is it his money they are throwing away on chicken? Then he remembers that he had not left them any money. He wonders if they have stolen the chicken, and becomes perturbed. He preaches and admonishes, scolds and cusses, but now he gets no response from the boys. They do not bother themselves about telling him where they got the chicken, but let him go on. He makes long speeches and exhausts his forces. Finally he begs and implores.

"I beseech you to tell me the truth. I will forgive you, no matter what you have done, if you will tell the truth!"

Now the boys can hold in no longer. Father hears a

79

spluttering sound. They throw off the quilts and sit up, and he notices that they are purple in the face from suppressed laughter. And as they can laugh now without restraint, Lennart says between the paroxysms, "Mother put a chicken in the food sack which she gave us when we left home."

Father draws himself up, looks at the boys, wants to speak, but finds no suitable words. He becomes even more majestic in his bearing, looks with withering scorn at them, and goes to his room without further parley.

It has dawned on Father how handy the boys are, and he makes use of this fact to escape hiring servants. Mornings he sends Lennart into the kitchen to make coffee and lets Hugo lay the breakfast table and fetch bread from the baker's. After breakfast he sits down on a chair and watches how the boys make up the beds, sweep the floors, and build a fire in the grate. He gives endless orders and sends them from one task to another, only to show his authority. When the morning chores are over, he goes out and remains away all the forenoon. The dinner he lets them fetch from a cooking school in the neighborhood. After dinner he leaves the boys for the evening, and exacts nothing more of them than that his bed shall be turned down when he comes home.

The boys are practically alone almost the entire day and can busy themselves in any way they choose.

One of their most important tasks is to write to their mother. They get letters from her every day, and she sends them paper and postage, so that they can answer her. Mother's letters are mostly admonitions that they be good to their father. She writes constantly of how lovable Father was when she first knew him, of how industrious and thrifty he was at the beginning of his career. They must be tender and kind to him. They must never forget how unhappy he is. "If you are very good to Father, per-

80

haps he may feel sorry for you and let you come home to me."

Mother tells them that she has called to see the dean and the burgomaster to ask if it were not possible to get back the boys. Both of them had replied that there was no help for her. The boys would have to stay with their father. Mother wants to move to Stockholm so that she may see her boys once in a while, at least, but everyone advises her to have patience and bide her time. They think Father will soon tire of the boys and send them home. Mother doesn't quite know what she should do. On the one hand, she thinks it dreadful that the boys are living in Stockholm with no one to look after them, and on the other hand, she knows that if she were to leave her home and her work, she could not take them and support them, even if they were freed. But for Christmas, at all events, Mother is coming to Stockholm to look after them.

The boys write and tell her what they do all day, hour by hour. They let Mother know that they cook for Father and make his bed. She apprehends that they are trying to be kind to him for her sake, but she probably perceives that they like him no better now than formerly.

Her little boys appear to be always alone. They live in a large city, where there are lots of people, but no one asks after them. And perhaps it is better thus. Who can tell what might happen to them were they to make any acquaintances?

They always beg of her not to be uneasy about them. They tell how they darn their stockings and sew on their buttons. They also intimate that Lennart has made great headway with his invention and say that when this is finished, all will be well.

Mother lives in a state of continual fear. Night and day her thoughts are with her boys. Night and day she prays to God to watch over her little sons, who live alone in a great city with no one to shield them from the temptations of the destroyer, and to keep their young hearts from the

81

desire for evil.

Father and the boys are sitting one morning at the opera. One of Father's old comrades, who is with the Royal Orchestra, has invited him to be present at a symphony rehearsal, and Father has taken the boys along. When the orchestra strikes up and the auditorium is filled with tone, Father is so affected that he can't control himself, and begins to weep. He sobs and blows his nose and moans aloud, time and again. He puts no restraint upon his feelings, but makes such a noise that the musicians are disturbed. A guard comes along and beckons him away, and Father takes the boys by the hand and slinks out without a word of protest. All the way home his tears continue to flow.

Father is walking on with a boy on each side, and he has kept their hands in his all the while. Suddenly the boys start crying. They understand now for the first time how much Father has loved his art. It was painful for him to sit there, besotted and broken, and listen to others playing. They feel sorry for him who had never become what he might have been. It was with Father as it might be with Lennart were he never to finish his flying-machine, or with Hugo if he were not to make any voyages of discovery. Think—if they should one day sit like old good-for-nothings and see fine airships sailing over their heads which they had not invented and were not allowed to pilot!

The boys were sitting one morning on opposite sides of the writing table. Father had taken a music roll under his arm and gone out. He had mumbled something about giving a music lesson, but the boys had not for a moment been tempted into believing this true.

Father is in an ugly mood as he walks up the street. He noticed the look the boys exchanged when he said that

82

he was going to a music lesson. "They are setting themselves up as judges of their father," he thinks. "I am too indulgent toward them. I should have given them each a sound box on the ear. It's their mother, I dare say, who is setting them against me. Suppose I were to keep an eye on the fine gentlemen?" he continues. "It would do no harm to find out how they attend to their lessons."

He turns back, walks quietly across the court, opens the door very softly, and stands in the boys' room without either of them having heard him coming. The boys jump up, red in the face, and Lennart quickly snatches a bundle of papers which he throws into the table drawer.

When the boys had been in Stockholm a day or two, they had asked which school they were to attend, and the father had replied that their school-going days were over now. He would try and procure a private tutor who would teach them. This proposition he had never carried into effect, nor had the boys said anything more about going to school. But in less than a week a school chart was discovered hanging on the wall in the boys' room. The school books had been brought forth, and every morning they sat on opposite sides of an old writing table and studied their lessons aloud. It was evident that they had received letters from their mother counseling them to try and study, so as not to forget entirely what they had learned.

Now, as Father unexpectedly comes into the room, he goes up to the chart first and studies it. He takes out his watch and compares. "Wednesday, between ten and eleven, geography." Then he comes up to the table. "Shouldn't you have geography at this hour?"

"Yes," the boys reply, growing flame-red in the face.

"Have you the geography and the map?"

The boys glance over at the book shelf and look confused. "We haven't begun yet," says Lennart.

"Indeed!" says Father. "You must have been up to something else." He straightens up, thoroughly pleased with himself. He has an advantage, which he doesn't care

83

to let go until he has browbeaten them very effectually.

Both boys are silent. Ever since the day they accompanied Father to the opera, they have felt sympathy for him, and it has not been such an effort for them to be kind to him as it was before. But, naturally, they haven't for a moment thought of taking Father into their confidence. He has not risen, in their estimation, although they are sorry for him.

"Were you writing letters?" father asks in his severest tone.

"No," say both boys at the same time.

"What were you doing?"

"Oh, just talking."

"That isn't true. I saw that Lennart hid something in the drawer of the table."

Now both boys are mum again.

"Take it out!" shouts the father, purple with rage. He thinks the sons have written to his wife, and, since they don't care to show the letter, of course there is something mean about him in it.

The boys do not stir, and Father raises his hand to strike Lennart, who is sitting before the table drawer.

"Don't touch him!" cries Hugo. "We were only talking over something which Lennart has invented."

Hugo pushes Lennart aside, opens the drawer, and pulls out the paper, which is scrawled full of airships of the most extraordinary shapes. "Last night Lennart thought out a new kind of sail for his airship. It was of this we were speaking."

Father wouldn't believe him. He bends over, searches in the drawer, but finds only sheets of paper covered with drawings of balloons, parachutes, flying-machines, and everything else appertaining to air-sailing.

To the great surprise of the boys, Father does not cast this aside at once, nor does he laugh at their attempts, but examines closely sheet after sheet. As a matter of fact, Father, too, has a little leaning toward mechanics, and was interested in things of this sort in days gone by, when his brain was still good for something. Soon he begins to ask questions as to the meaning of one thing and another, and, inasmuch as his words betray that, he is deeply interested and understands what he sees. Lennart fights his bashfulness, and answers him, hesitatingly at first and then more willingly.

Soon Father and boys are absorbed in a profound discussion about airships and air-sailing. After they are fairly well started, the boys chatter unreservedly and give Father a share in their plans and dreams of greatness. And while the father comprehends, of course, that the boys cannot fly very far with the airship which they have constructed, he is very much impressed. His little sons talk of aluminum motors, aeroplanes, and balancers, as though they were the simplest things in the world. He had thought them regular blockheads because they didn't get on very fast at school. Now, all at once, he believes they are a pair of little scientists.

The high-soaring thoughts and aspirations Father understands better than anything else; he recognizes them. He himself has dreamed in the same way, and he has no desire to laugh at such dreams.

Father doesn't go out again that morning, but sits and chats with the boys until it is time to fetch the food for dinner and set the table. And at that meal, Father and the boys are real good friends—to their great and mutual astonishment.

The hour is eleven at night, and Father is staggering up the street. The little boys are walking on either side of him; he holds their hands tightly clasped in his all the while.

They have sought him out in one of his haunts, where they have stationed themselves just inside the door. Father sits by himself at a table with a big brown toddy in front of him, and listens to a ladies' orchestra which is playing at the other end of the hall. After a moment's hesitancy, he rises reluctantly and goes over to the boys. "What is it?" he asks. "Why do you come here?"

"Father was to come home," they say. "This is the fifth of December. Father promised—"

Then he remembers that Lennart had confided to him that it was Hugo's birthday and that he had promised him to come home early. But this he had entirely forgotten. Hugo was probably expecting a birthday present from him, but he had not remembered to get him one.

At any rate, he has gone with the boys and is walking along, displeased with them and with himself. When he comes home, the birthday table is laid. The boys had wished to give a little party. Lennart had creamed some pancakes, which are now a few hours old and look like pieces of leather. They had received a little money from their mother, and with this they had bought nuts, raisins, and a bottle of soda water.

This fine feast they did not care to enjoy all by themselves, and they had been sitting and waiting for Father to come home and share it with them. Now, since they and Father have become friends, they cannot celebrate such a big event without him. Father understands it all, and the thought of being missed flatters him and puts him in a fairly good humor. Half-full as he is, he plumps himself down at the table. Just as he is about to take his place he stumbles, clutches at the tablecloth, falls, and draws down on the floor everything on the table. As he raises himself, he sees how the soda flows out over the floor and pickles and pancakes are strewn about among bits of porcelain and broken glass.

Father glances at the boys' long faces, rips out an oath, and makes a rush for the door, and he doesn't come back home until on towards morning.

One morning in February, the boys are coming up the street with their skates dangling from their shoulders.

They are not quite like themselves. They have grown thin and pale and look untidy and uncared for. Their hair is uncut; they are not well washed, and they have holes in both stockings and shoes. When they address each other, they use a lot of street-boy expressions, and one and another oath escapes from their lips.

A change has taken place in the boys. It had its beginning on the evening when their father forgot to come home to help celebrate Hugo's birthday. It was as if, until that time, they had been kept up by the hope that soon their father would be a changed man.

At first, they had counted on his tiring of them and sending them home. Later, they had fancied that he would become fond of them and give up drinking for their sakes, and they had even imagined that Mother and he might become reconciled, and that all of them would be happy. But it dawned upon them, that night, that Father was impossible. He could love nothing but drink. Even if he were kind to them for a little while, he didn't really care for them.

A heavy hopelessness fell upon the boys; nothing would ever be changed for them. They should never get away from Father. They felt as though they were doomed to sit shut in a dark prison all their lives. Not even their great plans for the future could comfort them. In the way that they were bound down, these plans could never be carried out. Only think, they were not learning anything! They knew enough of the histories of great men to know that he who wants to accomplish anything noteworthy must first of all have knowledge.

Still the hardest blow was that Mother did not come to them at Christmas. In the beginning of December, she had fallen down stairs and broken her leg, and was forced to lie in a hospital during the Christmas holidays; therefore, she could not come to Stockholm. Now that Mother was up, her school had begun again. Apart from this, she had no money with which to travel. The little that she had saved was spent while she lay ill.

The boys felt themselves deserted by the whole world. It was obvious that it never would be any better for them, no matter how good they were! So, gradually, they ceased to exert themselves with the sort of things that were tiresome. They might just as well do that which amused them.

The boys began to shirk their morning studies. No one heard their lessons, so what was the use of their studying? There had been good skating for a couple of days, and they might as well play truant all day. On the ice, there were always throngs of boys, and they had made the acquaintance of a number who also preferred skating to being shut in the house with their books.

It has turned out to be such a fine day that it is impossible to think of staying indoors. The weather is so clear and sunny that the school children have been granted skating leave. The whole street is filled with children, who have been home to get their skates and are now hurrying down to the ice.

The boys, as they move among the other children, appear solemn and low-spirited. Not a smile lights up their faces. Their misfortune is so heavy that they cannot forget it for a second.

When they come down on the ice, it is full of life and movement. All along the edges it is bordered with a tight mass of people; farther out, the skaters circle around one another like gnats, and still farther out, solitary black specks that float along at lightning speed are seen.

The boys buckle on their skates and join the other skaters. They skate very well, and as they glide out on the ice, full-speed, they get color in their cheeks and their eyes sparkle, but not for a moment do they appear happy like other children.

All of a sudden, as they are making a turn toward land, they catch sight of something very pretty. A big balloon comes from the direction of Stockholm and is sailing out toward Salt Lake. It is striped in reds and yellows, and when the sun strikes it, it glitters like a ball of fire. The basket is decorated with many-hued flags, and as the balloon does not fly very high, the bright color-play can be seen quite plainly.

When the boys spy the balloon, they send up a shriek of delight. It is the first time in their lives that they have seen a big balloon sailing through the air. All the dreams and plans which have been their consolation and joy during the many trying days come back to them when they see it. They stand still so that they may observe how the ropes and lines are fastened, and they take note of the anchor and the sand bags on the edge of the car.

The balloon moves with good speed over the ice-bound fjord. All the skaters, big and little, dart around one another, laughing and hooting at it when it first comes into sight, and then they bound after it. They follow it out to sea, in a long swaying line, like a drag line. The air-sailors amuse themselves by scattering handfuls of paper strips in a variety of colors, which come circling down slowly through the blue air.

The boys are foremost in the long line that is chasing after the balloon. They hurry forward, with heads thrown back, and gaze steadily turned upward. Their eyes dance with delight for the first time since they parted from their mother. They are beside themselves with excitement over the airship and think of nothing else than to follow it as long as possible.

But the balloon moves ahead rapidly, and one has to be a good skater not to be left behind. The crowd chasing after it thins down, but in the lead of those who keep up the pursuit the two little boys are seen. Afterwards people said there was something strange about them. They neither laughed nor shouted, but on their upturned faces there was a look of transport—as though they had seen a heavenly vision.

The balloon also affects the boys like a celestial guide, who has come to lead them back to the right path and teach them how to go forward with renewed courage. When the boys see it, their hearts bound with longing to begin work again on the great invention. Once more, they feel confident and happy. If only they are patient, they'll probably work their way toward success. A day will surely come when they can step into their own airship and soar aloft in space. Someday *they* will be the ones who travel up there, far above the people, and *their* airship will be more perfect than the one they now see. Theirs shall be an airship that can be steered and turned, lowered and raised, sail against wind and without wind. It shall carry them by day and by night, wherever they may wish to travel. They shall descend to the highest mountain peaks, travel over the dreariest deserts, and explore the most inaccessible regions. They shall behold all the glories of the world.

"It isn't worthwhile to lose heart, Hugo," says Lennart. "We'll have a fine time if we can only finish it!"

Father and his ill luck are things which do not concern them anymore. One, who has something as great to strive for as they have, cannot let himself be hindered by anything so pitiable!

The balloon gains in speed the farther out it comes. The skaters have ceased following it. The only ones who continue the chase are the two little boys. They move ahead as swiftly and lightly as if their feet had taken on wings.

Suddenly the people who stand on the shore and can look far out across the fjord send up a great cry of horror and fear. They see that the balloon, pursued all the while by the two children, sails away toward the fairway, where there is open sea. "Open sea! It is open sea out there!" the people shout.

The skaters down on the ice hear the shouts and turn their eyes toward the mouth of the fjord. They see how a strip of water shimmers in the sunlight yonder. They see, also, that two little boys are skating toward this strip,

90

which they do not notice because their eyes are fixed on the balloon, and, not for a second, do they turn them toward earth.

The people are calling out with all their might and stamping on the ice. Fast runners are hurrying on to stop them, but the little ones mark nothing of all this where they are chasing after the airship. They do not know that they alone are following it. They hear no cries back of them. They do not hear the splash and roar of the water ahead of them. They see only the balloon which, as it were, carries them with it. Lennart already feels his own airship rising under him, and Hugo soars away over the North Pole.

The people on the ice and on the shore see how rapidly they are nearing the open sea. For a second or two, they are in such breathless suspense that they can neither move nor cry out. It seems as if the two children are under a magic spell in their chase after a shining heavenly vision.

The air-sailors up in the balloon have also caught a glimpse of the little boys. They see that they are in danger and scream at them and make warning gestures, but the boys do not understand them. When they notice that the air-sailors are making signs at them, they think they want to take them up into the car. They stretch their arms toward them, overjoyed in the hope of accompanying them through the bright upper regions.

At this moment, the boys have reached the sailing channel, and, with arms uplifted, they skate down into the water and disappear without a cry for help. The skaters, who have tried to reach them in time, are standing a couple of seconds later on the edge of the ice, but the current has carried their bodies under the ice, and no helping hand can reach them.

The Wedding March

Now I'm going to tell a pretty story. A good many years ago there was to be a very big wedding at Svartsjö parish in Värmland.

First, there was to be a church ceremony, and after that, three days of feasting and merrymaking, and every day while the festivities lasted, there was to be dancing from early morning till far into the night.

Since there was to be so much dancing, it was of very great importance to get a good fiddler, and Juryman Nils Olafsson, who was managing the wedding, worried almost more over this than over anything else.

He did not care to engage the fiddler they had at Svartsjö. His name was Jan Öster. The juryman knew, to be sure, that he had quite a big name, but he was so poor that sometimes he would appear at a wedding in a frayed jacket and without shoes on his feet. The juryman didn't wish to see such a ragtag at the head of the bridal procession, so he decided to send a messenger to a musician in Jösse parish, who was commonly called Fiddler Mårten, and ask him if he wouldn't come and play at the wedding.

Fiddler Mårten didn't consider the proposition for a second, but promptly replied that he did not want to play at Svartsjö, because in that parish lived a musician who was more skilled than all others in Värmland. While they had him, there was no need for them to call another.

When Nils Olafsson received this answer, he took a few days to think it over, and then he sent word to a fiddler in Big Kil parish, named Olle in Säby, to ask him if he would not come and play at his daughter's wedding.

Olle in Säby answered in the same way as Fiddler Mårten. He sent his compliments to Nils Olafsson, and said that so long as there was such a capable musician as

Jan Öster to be had in Svartsjö, he didn't want to go there to play.

Nils Olafsson didn't like it that the musicians tried in this way to force upon him the very one he did not want. Now he considered that it was a point of honor with him to get another fiddler than Jan Öster.

A few days after he had the answer from Olle in Säby, he sent his servant to fiddler Lars Larsson, who lived at the game lodge in Ullerud parish. Lars Larsson was a well-to-do man who owned a fine farm. He was sensible and considerate and no hot spur, like the other musicians. But Lars Larsson, like the others, at once thought of Jan Öster, and asked how it happened that he was not to play at the wedding.

Nils Olafsson's servant thought it best to say to him that, since Jan Öster lived at Svartsjö, they could hear him play at any time. As Nils Olafsson was making ready to give a grand wedding, he wished to treat his guests to something a little better and more select.

"I doubt if you can get anyone better," said Lars Larsson.

"Now you must be thinking of answering in the same way as fiddler Mårten and Olle in Säby did," said the servant. Then he told him how he had fared with them.

Lars Larsson paid close attention to the servant's story, and then he sat quietly for a long while and pondered. Finally he answered in the affirmative: "Tell your master that I thank him for his invitation and will come."

The following Sunday, Lars Larsson journeyed down to Svartsjö. He drove up to the church knoll just as the wedding guests were forming into line to march to the church. He came driving in his own chaise, with a good horse and dressed in black broadcloth. He took out his fiddle from a highly polished box. Nils Olafsson received him effusively, thinking that here was a fiddler of whom he might be proud.

Immediately after Lars Larsson's arrival, Jan Öster,

93

too, came marching up to the church, with his fiddle under his arm. He walked straight up to the crowd around the bride, exactly as if he were asked to come and play at the wedding.

Jan Öster had come in the old gray homespun jacket which they had seen him wearing for ages. But, as this was to be such a grand wedding, his wife had made an attempt at mending the holes at the elbow by sewing big green patches over them. Jan Öster was a tall handsome man, and would have made a fine appearance at the head of the bridal procession, had he not been so shabbily dressed, and had his face not been so lined and seamed by worries and the hard struggle with misfortune.

When Lars Larsson saw Jan Öster coming, he seemed a bit displeased. "So you have called Jan Öster, too," he said under his breath to Juryman Nils Olafsson, "but at a grand wedding there's no harm in having two fiddlers."

"I did not invite him, that's certain!" protested Nils Olafsson. "I can't comprehend why he has come. Just wait, and I'll let him know that he has no business here!"

"Then some practical joker must have bidden him," said Lars Larsson. "But if you care to be guided by my counsel, appear as if nothing were wrong and go over and bid him welcome. I have heard said that he is a quick-tempered man, and who knows but he may begin to quarrel and fight if you were to tell him that he was not invited?"

This the juryman knew, too! It was no time to begin fussing when the bridal procession was forming on the church grounds; so he walked up to Jan Öster and bade him be welcome. Thereupon the two fiddlers took their places at the head of the procession. The bridal pair walked under a canopy; the bridesmaids and the groomsmen marched in pairs, and after them came the parents and relatives; so the procession was both imposing and long.

When everything was in readiness, a groomsman stepped up to the musicians and asked them to play the

94

Wedding March. Both musicians swung their fiddles up to their chins, but beyond that they did not get. And thus they stood! It was an old custom in Svartsjö for the best fiddler to strike up the Wedding March and to lead the music.

The groomsman looked at Lars Larsson, as though he were waiting for him to start; but Lars Larsson looked at Jan Öster and said, "It is you, Jan Öster, who must begin."

It did not seem possible to Jan Öster that the other fiddler, who was as finely dressed as any gentleman, should not be better than himself, who had come in his old homespun jacket straight from the wretched hovel where there were only poverty and distress. "No, indeed!" said he. "No, indeed!"

He saw that the bridegroom put forth his hand and touched Lars Larsson. "Larsson shall begin," said he.

When Jan Öster heard the bridegroom say this, he promptly lowered his fiddle and stepped aside.

Lars Larsson, on the other hand, did not move from the spot, but remained standing in his place, confident and pleased with himself. Nor did he raise the bow. "It is Jan Öster who shall begin," he repeated stubbornly and resistingly, as one who is used to having his own way.

There was some commotion among the crowd over the cause of the delay. The bride's father came forward and begged Lars Larsson to begin. The sexton stepped to the door of the church and beckoned to them to hurry along. The parson stood waiting at the altar.

"You can ask Jan Öster to begin, then," said Lars Larsson. "We musicians consider him to be the best among us."

"That may be so," said a peasant, "but we peasants consider you the best one."

Then the other peasants also gathered around them. "Well, begin, why don't you?" they said. "The parson is waiting. We'll become a laughing-stock to the church people."

95

Lars Larsson stood there quite as stubborn and determined as before. "I can't see why the parish people are so opposed to having their own fiddler placed in the lead."

Nils Olafsson was perfectly furious because Jan Öster had been forced upon him in this way. He came close up to Lars Larsson and whispered: "I comprehend that it is you who have called hither Jan Öster, and that you have arranged this to do him honor. But be quick, now, and play up, or I'll drive that ragamuffin from the church grounds in disgrace and by force!"

Lars Larsson looked him square in the face and nodded to him without displaying any irritation. "Yes, you are right in saying that we must have an end of this," said he.

He beckoned to Jan Öster to return to his place. Then he himself walked forward a step or two, and turned around that all might see him. Then he flung the bow far from him, pulled out his case-knife, and cut all four violin strings, which snapped with a sharp twang. "It shall not be said that I count myself better than Jan Öster!" said he.

It appears that for three years Jan Öster had been musing on an air which he couldn't get out over the strings, because at home he was bound down by dull, gray cares and worries, and nothing ever happened to him, either great or small, to lift him above the daily grind. But when he heard Lars Larsson's strings snap, he threw back his head and filled his lungs. His features were rapt, as though he were listening to something far away; and then he began to play. And the air, which he had been musing over for three years, became all at once dear to him, and as the tones of it vibrated, he walked with proud step down to the church.

The bridal procession had never before heard an air like that! It carried them along with such speed that not even Nils Olafsson could think of staying back. And everyone was so pleased both with Jan Öster and with Lars Larsson that the entire following entered the church, their eyes brimming with tears of joy.

The Musician

No one in Ullerud could say anything of fiddler Lars Larsson but that he was both meek and modest in his later years. But he had not always been thus, it seems. In his youth, he had been so overbearing and boastful that people were in despair about him. It is said that he was changed and made over in a single night, and this is the way it happened.

Lars Larsson went out for a stroll late one Saturday night, with his fiddle under his arm. He was excessively gay and jovial, for he had just come from a party where his playing had tempted both young and old to dance. He walked along, thinking that while his bow was in motion no one had been able to sit still. There had been such a whirl in the cabin that once or twice he fancied the chairs and tables were dancing too! "I verily believe they have never before had a musician like me in these parts," he remarked to himself. "But I had a mighty rough time of it before I became such a clever chap!" he continued. "When I was a child, it was no fun for me when my parents put me to tending cows and sheep and when I forgot everything else to sit and twang my fiddle. And just fancy! they wouldn't so much as give me a real violin. I had nothing to play on but an old wooden box over which I had stretched some strings. In the daytime, when I could be alone in the woods, I fared rather well; but it was none too cheerful to come home in the evening when the cattle had strayed from me! Then I heard often enough, from both Father and Mother, that I was a good-for-nothing and never would amount to anything."

In that part of the forest where Lars Larsson was strolling, a little river was trying to find its way. The ground was stony and hilly, and the stream had great difficulty in getting ahead, winding this way and that way, rolling over little falls and rapids—and yet it appeared to get nowhere. The path where the fiddler walked, on the other hand, tried to go as straight ahead as possible. Therefore, it was continually meeting the sinuous stream, and each time it would dart across it by using a little bridge. The musician also had to cross the stream repeatedly, and he was glad of it. He thought it was as though he had found company in the forest.

Where he was tramping, it was light summer night. The sun had not yet come up, but its being away made no difference, for it was as light as day all the same.

Still the light was not quite what it is in the daytime. Everything had a different color. The sky was perfectly white, the trees and the growths on the ground were grayish, but everything was as distinctly visible as in the daytime, and when Lars Larsson paused on any of the numerous bridges and looked down into the stream, he could distinguish every ripple on the water.

"When I see a stream like this in the wilderness," he thought, "I am reminded of my own life. As persistent as this stream have I been in forcing my way past all that has obstructed my path. Father has been my rock ahead, and Mother tried to hold me back and bury me between moss tufts, but I stole past both of them and got out in the world. Heigh-ho, hie, hie! I think Mother is still sitting at home and weeping for me. But what do I care! She might have known that I should amount to something some day, instead of trying to oppose me!"

Impatiently he tore some leaves from a branch and threw them into the river.

"Look! thus have I torn myself loose from everything at home," he said, as he watched the leaves borne away by the water. "I am just wondering if Mother knows that I'm the best musician in Värmland?" he remarked as he went farther.

He walked on rapidly until he came across the stream

98

again. Then he stopped and looked into the water.

Here the river went along in a struggling rapid, creating a terrible racket. As it was night, one heard from the stream sounds quite different from those of the daytime, and the musician was perfectly astonished when he stood still and listened. There was no bird song in the trees and no music in the pines and no rustling in the leaves. No wagon wheels creaked in the road and no cowbells tinkled in the wood. One heard only the rapids; but because all the other things were hushed, it could be heard so much better than during the day. It sounded as though everything thinkable and unthinkable was rioting and clamoring in the depths of the stream. First, it sounded as if someone were sitting down there and grinding grain between stones, and then it sounded as though goblets were clinking in a drinking bout; and again there was a murmuring, as when the congregation had left the church and were standing on the church knoll after the service, talking earnestly together.

"I suppose this, too, is a kind of music," thought the fiddler, "although I can't find anything much in it! I think the air that I composed the other day was much more worth listening to."

But the longer Lars Larsson listened to the music of the rapid, the better he thought it sounded.

"I believe you are improving," he said to the rapid. "It must have dawned upon you that the best musician in Värmland is listening to you!"

The instant he had made this remark, he fancied he heard a couple of clear metallic sounds, as when someone picks a violin string to hear if it is in tune.

"But see, hark! The Water Sprite himself has arrived. I can hear how he begins to thrum on the violin. Let us hear now if you can play better than I!" said Lars Larsson, laughing. "But I can't stand here all night waiting for you to begin," he called to the water. "Now I must be going; but I promise you that I will also stop at the next bridge and listen, to hear if you can cope with me."

He went farther and, as the stream in its winding course ran into the wood, he began thinking once more of his home.

"I wonder how the little brooklet that runs by our house is getting on? I should like to see it again. I ought to go home once in a while, to see if Mother is suffering want and hardship since Father's death. But busy as I am, it is almost impossible. As busy as I am just now, I say, I can't look after anything but the fiddle. There is hardly an evening in the week that I am at liberty."

In a little while, he met the stream again, and his thoughts were turned to something else. At this crossing the river did not come rushing on in a noisy rapid, but glided ahead rather quietly. It lay perfectly black and shiny under the night-gray forest trees, and carried with it one and another patch of snow-white scum from the rapids above.

When the musician came down upon the bridge and heard no sound from the stream but a soft swish now and then, he began to laugh.

"I might have known that the Water Sprite wouldn't care to come to the meeting," he shouted. "To be sure, I have always heard that he is considered an excellent performer, but one who lies still forever in a brook and never hears anything new can't know very much! He perceives, no doubt, that here stands one who knows more about music than he, therefore he doesn't care to let me hear him."

Then he went farther and lost sight of the river again. He came into a part of the forest which he had always thought dismal and bleak to wander through. There the ground was covered with big stone heaps, and gnarled pine stumps lay uprooted among them. If there was anything magical or fearsome in the forest, one would naturally think that it concealed itself here.

When the musician came in among the wild stone

blocks, a shudder passed through him, and he began to wonder if it had not been unwise of him to boast in the presence of the Water Sprite. He fancied the large pine roots began to gesticulate, as if they were threatening him. "Beware, you who think yourself cleverer than the Water Sprite!" it seemed as if they wanted to say.

Lars Larsson felt how his heart contracted with dread. A heavy weight bore down upon his chest, so that he could scarcely breathe, and his hands became ice-cold. Then he stopped in the middle of the wood and tried to talk sense to himself.

"Why, there's no musician in the waterfall!" said he. "Such things are only superstition and nonsense! It's of no consequence what I have said or haven't said to him."

As he spoke, he looked around him, as if for some confirmation of the truth of what he said. Had it been daytime, every tiny leaf would have winked at him that there was nothing dangerous in the wood; but now, at night, the leaves on the trees were closed and silent and looked as though they were hiding all sorts of dangerous secrets.

Lars Larsson grew more and more alarmed. That which caused him the greatest fear was having to cross the stream once more before it and the road parted company and went in different directions. He wondered what the Water Sprite would do to him when he walked across the last bridge—if he might perhaps stretch a big black hand out of the water and drag him down into the depths.

He had worked himself into such a state of fright that he thought of turning back. But then he would meet the stream again. And if he were to turn out of the road and go into the wood, he would also meet it, the way it kept bending and winding itself!

He felt so nervous that he didn't know what to do. He was snared and captured and bound by that stream, and saw no possibility of escape.

Finally he saw before him the last bridge crossing. Directly opposite him, on the other side of the stream, stood an old mill, which must have been abandoned these many years. The big mill wheel hung motionless over the water. The sluice gate lay mouldering on the land; the mill race was moss-grown, and its sides were lined with common fern and beard-moss.

"If all had been as formerly and there were people here," thought the musician, "I should be safe now from all danger."

But, at all events, he felt reassured in seeing a building constructed by human hands, and, as he crossed the stream, he was scarcely frightened at all. Nor did anything dreadful happen to him. The Water Sprite seemed to have no quarrel with him. He was simply amazed to think he had worked himself into a panic over nothing whatever.

He felt very happy and secure, and became even happier when the mill door opened and a young girl came out to him. She looked like an ordinary peasant girl. She had a cotton kerchief on her head and wore a short skirt and full jacket, but her feet were bare.

She walked up to the musician and said to him without further ceremony, "If you will play for me, I'll dance for you."

"Why, certainly," said the fiddler, who was in fine spirits now that he was rid of his fear. "That I can do, of course. I have never in my life refused to play for a pretty girl who wants to dance."

He took his place on a stone near the edge of the millpond, raised the violin to his chin, and began to play.

The girl took a few steps in rhythm with the music; then she stopped. "What kind of a polka are you playing?" said she. "There is no vim in it."

The fiddler changed his tune; he tried one with more life in it.

The girl was just as dissatisfied. "I can't dance to such a draggy polka," said she.

Then Lars Larsson struck up the wildest air he knew.

"If you are not satisfied with this one," he said, "you will have to call hither a better musician than I am."

The instant he said this, he felt that a hand caught his arm at the elbow and began to guide the bow and increase the tempo. Then from the violin there poured forth a strain the like of which he had never before heard. It moved in such a quick tempo he thought that a rolling wheel couldn't have kept up with it.

"Now, that's what I call a polka!" said the girl, and began to swing round.

But the musician did not glance at her. He was so astonished at the air he was playing that he stood with closed eyes, to hear better. When he opened his eyes, after a moment, the girl was gone. But he did not wonder much at this. He continued to play on, long and well, only because he had never before heard such violin playing.

"It must be time now to finish with this," he thought finally, and wanted to lay down the bow. But the bow kept up its motion; he couldn't make it stop. It traveled back and forth over the strings and jerked the hand and arm with it, and the hand that held the neck of the violin and fingered the strings could not free itself either.

The cold sweat stood out on Lars Larsson's brow, and he was frightened now in earnest.

"How will this end? Shall I sit here and play till doomsday?" he asked himself in despair.

The bow ran on and on, and magically called forth one tune after another. Always it was something new, and it was so beautiful that the poor fiddler must have known how little his own skill was worth. And it was this that tortured him worse than the fatigue.

"He who plays upon my violin understands the art. But never in all my born days have I been anything but a bungler. Now, for the first time, I'm learning how music should sound."

For a few seconds he became so transported by the music that he forgot his evil fate; then he felt how his arm ached from weariness, and he was seized anew with despair.

"This violin I cannot lay down until I have played myself to death. I can understand that the Water Sprite won't be satisfied with less."

He began to weep over himself, but all the while he kept on playing.

"It would have been better for me had I stayed at home in the little cabin with Mother. What is all the glory worth if it is to end in this way?"

He sat there hour after hour. Morning came on; the sun rose, and the birds sang all around him, but he played and he played without intermission.

As it was a Sunday that dawned, he had to sit there by the old mill all alone. No human beings tramped in this part of the forest. They went to church down in the dale and to the villages along the big highway.

Forenoon came along, and the sun stepped higher and higher in the sky. The birds grew silent, and the wind began to murmur in the long pine needles.

Lars Larsson did not let the summer day's heat deter him. He played and played. At last, evening was ushered in, the sun sank, but his bow needed no rest, and his arm continued to move.

"It is absolutely certain that this will be the death of me!" said he. "And it is a righteous punishment for all my conceit."

Far along in the evening, a human being came wandering through the wood. It was a poor old woman with bent back and white hair, and a countenance that was furrowed by many sorrows.

"It seems strange," thought the player, "but I think I recognize that old woman. Can it be possible that it is my mother? Can it be possible that Mother has grown so old and gray?"

He called aloud and stopped her: "Mother, Mother, come here to me!" he cried.

She paused, as if unwillingly. "I hear now with my own ears that you are the best musician in Värmland," said she. "I can well understand that you do not care any more for a poor old woman like me!"

"Mother, Mother, don't pass me by!" cried Lars Larsson. "I'm no great performer—only a poor wretch. Come here that I may speak with you!"

Then the mother came nearer and saw how he sat and played. His face was as pale as death, his hair dripped sweat, and blood oozed out from under the roots of his nails.

"Mother, I have fallen into misfortune because of my vanity, and now I must play myself to death. But tell me, before this happens, if you can forgive me—who left you alone and poor in your old age!"

His mother was seized with a great compassion for the son, and all the anger she had felt toward him was as if blown away. "Why, surely I forgive you!" said she. And as she saw his anguish and bewilderment and wanted him to understand that she meant what she said, she repeated it in the name of God.

"In the name of God our Redeemer, I forgive you!"

And when she said this, the bow stopped; the violin fell to the ground, and the musician arose—saved and redeemed. For the enchantment was broken, because his old mother had felt such compassion for his distress that she had spoken God's name over him.

A Story from Halstanäs

In olden times there stood by the roadside an old country house called Halstanäs. It was comprised of a long row of red-painted houses, which were of low structure, and right behind them lay the forest. Close to the dwelling-house was a large wild cherry tree, which showered its black fruit over the red-tiled roof. A bell under a small belfry hung over the gable of the stables.

Just outside the kitchen door was a dovecote with a neat little trelliswork outside the holes. From the attic, a cage for squirrels was hanging; it consisted of two small green houses and a large wheel, and in front of a big hedge of lilacs stood a long row of beehives covered with bark.

There was a pond belonging to the farm, full of fat carp and slim water snakes; there was also a kennel at the entrance; there were white gates at the end of the avenue, and at the garden walks, and in every place where they could possibly have a gate. There were big lofts with dark lumber rooms, where old-fashioned uniforms and ladies' headgear, a hundred years old, were stored away; there were large chests full of silk gowns and bridal finery; there were old pianos and violins, guitars and bassoons. In bureaus and cabinets were manuscript songs and old yellow letters; on the walls of the entrance hall hung guns, pistols and hunting bags; on the floor were rugs, in which patches of old silken gowns were woven together with pieces of threadbare cotton curtains. There was a large porch, where the deadly nightshade, summer after summer, grew up a thin trelliswork; there were large, yellow front doors, which were fastened with bolts and catches; the hall was strewn with sprigs of juniper, and the windows had small panes and heavy wooden shutters.

One summer old Colonel Beerencreutz came on a visit

to this house. It is supposed to have been the very year after he left Ekeby. At that time, he had taken rooms at a farm at Svartsjö, and it was only on rare occasions that he went visiting. He still had his horse and gig, but he scarcely ever used them. He said that he had grown old in earnest and that home was the best place for old people.

Beerencreutz was also loath to leave the work he had in hand. He was weaving rugs for his two rooms—large, many-colored rugs in a rich and strangely-thought-out pattern. It took him an endless time, because he had his own way of weaving, for he used no loom, but stretched his wool from the one wall to the other right across the one room. He did this in order to see the whole rug at one time. But to cross the woof and afterwards bring the threads together to a firm web was no easy matter. And then there was the pattern, which he himself thought out, and the colors which should match. This took the Colonel more time than anyone would have imagined; for while Beerencreutz was busy getting the pattern right, and while he was working with warp and woof, he often sat and thought of God. Our Lord, he thought, was likewise sitting at a loom, still larger, and with an even more peculiar pattern to weave. And he knew that there must be both light and dark shades in that weaving. But Beerencreutz would at times sit and think so long about this, until he fancied he saw before him his own life and the life of the people whom he had known, and with whom he had lived, forming a small portion of God's great weaving, and he seemed to see that piece so distinctly that he could discern both outlines and coloring. And if one asked Beerencreutz what the pattern in his work really meant, he would be obliged to confess that it was the life of himself and his friends which he wove into the rug as a faint imitation of what he thought he had seen represented on God's loom.

The Colonel, however, was accustomed to paying a visit to some old friends every year, just after midsummer. He had always liked best to travel through the country when the fields were still scented with clover, and blue and yellow flowers grew along the roadside in two long straight rows.

This year the Colonel had hardly got to the great highroad before he met his old friend, Ensign von Örneclou. And the Ensign, who was traveling about all the year round, and who knew all the country houses in Värmland, gave him some good advice.

"Go to Halstanäs and call upon Ensign Vestblad," he said to the Colonel. "I can only tell you, Old Man, I don't know a house in the whole country where one fares better."

"What Vestblad are you speaking about?" asked the Colonel. "I suppose you don't mean the old Ensign whom the Major's wife showed the door?"

"The very man," said the Ensign. "But Vestblad is not the same man he was. He has married a fine lady—a real stunning woman, Colonel—who has made a man of him. It was a wonderful piece of good luck for Vestblad that such a splendid girl should take a fancy to him. She was not exactly young any longer, but no more was he. You should go to Halstanäs, Colonel, and see what wonders love can work."

And the Colonel went to Halstanäs to see if Örneclou spoke the truth. He had, as a matter of fact, now and then wondered what had become of Vestblad; in his young days he had kicked so recklessly over the traces that even the Major's wife at Ekeby could not put up with him. She had not been able to keep him at Ekeby more than a couple of years before she was obliged to turn him out. Vestblad had become such a heavy drinker that a Cavalier could hardly associate with him. And now Örneclou declared that he owned a country house, and had made an excellent match.

The Colonel consequently went to Halstanäs, and saw at the first glance that it was a real old country-seat. He had only to look at the avenue of birches with all the names cut on the fine old trees. Such birches he had seen only at good old country houses. The Colonel drove slowly up to the house, and every moment his pleasure increased. He saw lime hedges of the proper kind, so close that one could walk on the top of them, and there were a couple of terraces with stone steps so old that they were half-buried in the ground. When the Colonel drove past the pond, he saw indistinctly the dark carp in the yellowish water. The pigeons flew up from the road flapping their wings; the squirrel stopped its wheel; the watchdog lay with its head on its paws, wagging its tail, and at the same time faintly growling. Close to the porch the Colonel saw an anthill, where the ants, unmolested, went to and fro, to and fro. He looked at the flower beds inside the grass border. There they grew, all the old flowers: narcissus and pyrola, sempervivum and marigold, and on the bank grew small white daisies, which had been there so long that they now sowed themselves like weeds. Beerencreutz again said to himself that this was indeed a real old country house, where both plants and animals and human beings thrived as well as could be.

When at last he drove up to the front door, he had as good a reception as he could wish for, and as soon as he had brushed the dust off him he was taken to the dining room, and he was offered plenty of good old-fashioned food—the same old cakes for dessert that his mother used to give him when he came home from school, and he had never tasted any so good elsewhere.

Beerencreutz looked with surprise at Ensign Vestblad. He went about quiet and content, with a long pipe in his mouth and a skullcap on his head. He wore an old morning coat, which he had difficulty in getting out of when it was time to dress for dinner. That was the only sign of the Bohemian left as far as Beerencreutz could see.

He went about and looked after his men, calculated their wages, saw how things were getting on in the fields and meadows, gathered a rose for his wife when he went through the garden, and he indulged no longer in either swearing or spitting. But what astonished the Colonel most of all was the discovery that old Ensign Vestblad kept his books. He took the Colonel into his office and showed him large books with red backs. And those he kept himself, he had lined with red ink and black ink, written the headings with large letters, and put down everything, even to a stamp.

But Ensign Vestblad's wife, who was a born lady, called Beerencreutz cousin, and they soon found out the relationship between them, and they talked all their relatives over. At last Beerencreutz became so intimate with Mrs. Vestblad, that he consulted her about the rug he was weaving.

It was a matter of course that the Colonel should stay the night. He was taken to the best spare room to the right of the hall and close to his host's bedroom, and his bed was a large four-poster with heaps of eiderdowns.

The Colonel fell asleep as soon as he got into bed, but awoke later on in the night. He immediately got out of bed and went and opened the window shutters. He had a view over the garden, and in the light summer night he could see all the gnarled old apple trees, with their worm-eaten leaves, and with numerous props under the decayed branches. He saw the large wild apple tree, which in the autumn would give barrels of inedible fruit; he saw the strawberries, which had just begun to ripen under their profusion of green leaves.

The Colonel stood and looked at it as if he could not afford to waste his time in sleeping. Outside his window at the peasant farm where he lived, all he could see was a stony hill and a couple of juniper bushes, and it was natural that a man like Beerencreutz should feel more at home amongst well-trimmed hedges and roses in bloom.

When in the quiet stillness of the night one looks out upon a garden, one often has a feeling that it is not real and natural. It can be so still that one can almost fancy oneself in the theater; one imagines that the trees are painted and the roses made of paper. And it was something like this the Colonel felt as he stood there. "It cannot be possible," he thought, "that all this is real. It can only be a dream." But then a few rose leaves fell softly to the ground from the big rose tree just outside his window, and he realized that everything was genuine. Everything was real and genuine; both day and night the same peace and contentment everywhere.

When he went and laid down again, he left the window shutters open. He lay in the high bed and looked time after time at the rose tree; it is impossible to describe his pleasure in looking at it. He thought what a strange thing it was that such a man as Vestblad should have this flower of paradise outside his window.

The more the Colonel thought of Vestblad, the more surprised he became that such a foal should end his days in such a stable. He was not good for much at the time he was turned away from Ekeby. Who would have thought he would have become a staid and well-to-do man?

The Colonel lay and laughed to himself, and wondered whether Vestblad still remembered how he used to amuse himself in the olden days when he was living at Ekeby. On dark and stormy nights, he used to rub himself over with phosphorus, mount a black horse, and ride over the hills to the ironworks, where the smiths and the workmen lived, and if anyone happened to look out his window and saw a horseman shining with a bluish-white light tearing past, he hastened to bar and bolt everywhere, saying it was best to say one's prayers twice that night, for the devil was abroad.

Oh, yes, to frighten simple folks by such tricks was a favorite amusement in olden days, but Vestblad had carried his jokes further than anyone else the Colonel knew.

An old woman of the parish had died at Viksta, which belonged to Ekeby. Vestblad happened to hear about this. He also heard that the corpse had been taken from the

111

house and placed in a barn. At night Vestblad put on his fiery array, mounted his black horse, and rode to the farmstead, and people there, who were about, had seen a fiery horseman ride up to the barn, where the corpse lay, ride three times around it and disappear through the door. They had also seen the horseman come out again, ride three times around the house and then disappear. But in the morning, when they went into the barn to see the corpse, it was gone, and they thought the devil had been there and carried her off. This supposition had been enough for them. But a couple of weeks later, they found the body, which had been thrown onto a hayloft in the barn, and then there was a great outcry. They found out who the fiery horseman was, and the peasants were on the watch to give Vestblad a good hiding. But the Major's wife would not have him at her table or in her house any longer; she packed his knapsack and asked him to betake himself elsewhere. And Vestblad went out into the world and made his fortune.

A strange feeling of uneasiness came over the Colonel as he lay in bed. He felt as if something were going to happen. He had hardly realized before what an ugly story it was. He had, no doubt, even laughed at it at the time. They had not been in the habit of taking much notice of what happened to a poor old pauper in those days, but, great God! how furious one would have been if anybody had done that to one's own mother!

A suffocating feeling came over the Colonel; he breathed heavily. The thought of what Vestblad had done appeared so vile and hateful to him, it weighed him down like a nightmare. He was half afraid of seeing the dead woman, of seeing her appear from behind the bed. He felt as if she must be quite near. And from the four corners of the room, the Colonel heard terrible words: "God will not forgive it! God has never forgotten it!"

The Colonel closed his eyes, but then he suddenly saw before him God's great loom, where the web was woven

112

with the fates of men, and he thought he saw Ensign Vestblad's square, and it was dark on three sides, and he, who understood something about weaving and patterns, knew that the fourth side would also have to be covered with the dark shade. It could not be done in any other way, otherwise there would be a mistake in the weaving.

A cold sweat broke out on his forehead; it seemed to him that he looked upon what was the hardest and most immovable in all the world. He saw how the fate which a man has worked out in his past life will pursue him to the end. And to think there were actually people who thought they could escape it!

Escape it! Escape! All was noted and written down; the one color and the one figure necessitated the other, and everything came about as it was bound to come about.

Suddenly Colonel Beerencreutz sat up in bed; he would look at the flowers and the roses, and think that perhaps our Lord could forget after all. But at the moment Beerencreutz sat up in bed, the bedroom door opened, and one of the farm laborers—a stranger to him—put his head in and nodded to the Colonel.

It was now so light that the Colonel saw the man quite distinctly. It was the most hideous face he had ever seen. He had small, gray eyes like a pig, a flat nose, and a thin, bristly beard. One could not say that the man looked like an animal, for animals nearly always have good faces, but still, he had something of the animal about him. His lower jaw projected; his neck was thick, and his forehead was quite hidden by his rough, unkempt hair.

He nodded three times to the Colonel, and, every time, his mouth opened with a broad grin, and he put out his hand, red with blood, and showed it triumphantly. Up to this moment, the Colonel had sat up in bed as if paralyzed, but now he jumped up and was at the door in two steps. But when he reached the door, the fellow was gone and the door closed.

The Colonel was just on the point of raising the alarm

when it struck him that the door must be fastened on the inside as he had himself locked it the night before, and on examining it, he found that it had not been unlocked. The Colonel felt almost ashamed to think that in his old age he had begun to see ghosts. He went straight back to bed.

When the morning came and he had breakfasted, the Colonel felt still more ashamed. He had excited himself to such an extent that he had trembled all over and perspired from fear. He said not a word about it. But later on in the day, he and Vestblad went over the estate. As they passed a laborer who was cutting sods on a bank, Beerencreutz recognized him again. It was the man he had seen in the night. He recognized feature for feature.

"I would not keep that man a day longer in my service, my friend," said Beerencreutz when they had walked a short distance. And he told Vestblad what he had seen in the night. "I tell you this simply to warn you, in order that you may dismiss the man."

But Vestblad would not; he was just the man he would not dismiss. And when Beerencreutz pressed him more and more, he at last confessed that he would not do anything to the man, because he was the son of an old pauper woman who had died at Viksta close to Ekeby.

"You no doubt remember the story?" he added. "If that's the case, I would rather go to the end of the world than live another day with that man about the place," said Beerencreutz. An hour after, he left, and was almost angry that his warning was not heeded. "Some misfortune will happen before I come here again," said the Colonel to Vestblad, as he took leave.

Next year, at the same time, the Colonel was preparing for another visit to Halstanäs. But before he got so far, he heard some sad news about his friends. As the clock struck one, a year after the very night he had slept there, Ensign Vestblad and his wife had been murdered in their bedroom by one of their laborers—a man with a neck like a bull, a flat nose, and eyes like a pig.

114

The Peace of God

Once upon a time there was an old farmhouse. It was Christmas Eve, the sky was heavy with snow, and the north wind was biting. It was just that time in the afternoon when everybody was busy finishing their work before they went to the bathhouse to have their Christmas bath. There they had made such a fire that the flames went right up the chimney, and sparks and soot were whirled about by the wind, and fell down on the snow-decked roofs of the outhouses. And as the flames appeared above the chimney of the bathhouse, and rose like a fiery pillar above the farm, everyone suddenly felt that Christmas was at hand. The girl that was scrubbing the entrance floor began to hum, although the water was freezing in the bucket beside her. The men in the woodshed who were cutting Christmas logs began to cut two at a time, and swung their axes as merrily as if log-cutting were a mere pastime.

An old woman came out of the pantry with a large pile of cakes in her arms. She went slowly across the yard into the large red-painted dwelling house, and carried the cakes carefully into the best room, and put them down on the long seat. Then she spread the tablecloth on the table, and arranged the cakes in heaps—a large and a small cake in each heap. She was a singularly ugly old woman, with reddish hair, heavy drooping eyelids, and with a peculiar strained look about the mouth and chin, as if the muscles were too short. But being Christmas Eve, there was such a joy and peace over her that one did not notice how ugly she was.

But there was one person on the farm who was not happy, and that was the girl who was tying up the whisks made of birch twigs that were to be used for the baths.

115

She sat near the fireplace, and had a whole armful of fine birch twigs laying beside her on the floor, but the twigs would not keep knotted. The best room had a narrow, low window, with small panes, and through them, the light from the bathhouse shone into the room, playing on the floor and gilding the birch twigs. But the higher the fire burned the more unhappy was the girl. She knew that the whisks would fall to pieces as soon as one touched them, and that she would never hear the last of it until the next Christmas fire was lighted.

Just as she sat there bemoaning herself, the person of whom she was most afraid came into the room. It was her master, Ingmar Ingmarson. He was sure to have been to the bathhouse to see if the stove was hot enough, and now he wanted to see how the whisks were coming. He was old, Ingmar Ingmarson, and he was fond of everything old, and just because people were beginning to leave off bathing in the bathhouses and being whipped with birch twigs, he made a great point of having it done on his farm, and having it done properly.

Ingmar Ingmarson wore an old coat of sheepskin, skin trousers, and shoes smeared over with pitch. He was dirty and unshaven, slow in all his movements, and came in so softly that one might very well have mistaken him for a beggar. His features resembled his wife's features, and his ugliness resembled his wife's ugliness, for they were relations. From the time the girl first began to notice anything, she had learned to feel a wholesome reverence for anybody who looked like that; for it was a great thing to belong to the old family of the Ingmars, which had always been the first in the village. But the highest to which a man could attain was to be Ingmar Ingmarson himself, and be the richest, the wisest, and the mightiest in the whole parish.

Ingmar Ingmarson went up to the girl, took one of the whisks, and swung it in the air. It immediately fell to pieces; one of the twigs landed on the Christmas table, another on the big four poster.

"I say, my girl," said old Ingmar, laughing, "do you think one uses that kind of whisk when one takes a bath at the Ingmar's, or are you very tender, my girl?"

When the girl saw that her master did not take it more seriously than that, she took heart, and answered that she could certainly make whisks that would not go to pieces if she could get proper withes to bind them with.

"Then I suppose I must try to get some for you, my girl," said old Ingmar, for he was in a real Christmas humor.

He went out of the room, stepped over the girl who was scouring the floor, and remained standing on the doorstep, to see if there were anyone about whom he could send to the birch wood for some withes. The farm hands were still busy cutting yule logs; his son came out of the barn with the Christmas sheaf; his two sons-in-law were putting the carts into the shed so that the yard could be tidy for the Christmas festival. None of them had time to leave their work.

The old man quietly made up his mind to go himself. He went across the yard as if he were going into the cowshed, looked cautiously around to make sure no one noticed him, and stole around outside the barn where there was a fairly good road to the wood. The old man thought it was better not to let anyone know where he was going, for either his son or his sons-in-law might then have begged him to remain at home, and old people like to have their own way.

He went down the road, across the fields, through the small pine forest into the birch wood. Here he left the road, and waded in the snow to find some young birches.

About the same time, the wind at last accomplished what it had been busy with the whole day: it tore the snow from the clouds, and now came rushing through the wood with a long train of snow after it.

Ingmar Ingmarson had just stooped down and cut off a

117

birch twig when the wind came tearing along laden with snow. Just as the old man was getting up, the wind blew a whole heap of snow in his face. His eyes were full of snow, and the wind whirled so violently around him that he was obliged to turn round once or twice.

The whole misfortune, no doubt, arose from Ingmar Ingmarson being so old. In his younger days, a snowstorm would certainly not have made him dizzy. But now everything danced round him as if he had joined in a Christmas polka, and when he wanted to go home, he went in the wrong direction. He went straight into the large pine forest behind the birch wood instead of going toward the fields.

It soon grew dark, and the storm continued to howl and whirl around him amongst the young trees on the outskirts of the forest. The old man saw quite well that he was walking amongst fir trees, but he did not understand that this was wrong, for there were also fir trees on the other side of the birch wood nearest the farm. But by-and-by, he got so far into the forest that everything was quiet and still—one could not feel the storm, and the trees were high with thick stems—then he found out that he had mistaken the road and would turn back.

He became excited and upset at the thought that he could lose his way, and as he stood there in the midst of the pathless wood, he was not sufficiently clearheaded to know in which direction to turn. He went first to the one side and then to the other. At last, it occurred to him to retrace his way in his own footprints, but darkness came on, and he could no longer follow them. The trees around him grew higher and higher. Whichever way he went, it was evident to him that he got further and further into the forest.

It was like witchcraft and sorcery, he thought, that he should be running about the woods like this all evening and be too late for the bathing. He turned his cap and rebound his garter, but his head was no clearer. It had become quite dark, and he began to think that he would have to remain the whole night in the woods.

He leaned against a tree, stood still for a little, and tried to collect his thoughts. He knew this forest so well, and had walked in it so much that he ought to know every single tree. As a boy he had gone there and tended sheep. He had gone there and laid snares for the birds. In his young days, he had helped to fell trees there. He had seen old trees cut down and new ones grow up. At last, he thought he had an idea where he was, and fancied if he went that way, he must come upon the right road, but all the same, he went deeper and deeper into the forest.

Once he felt smooth, firm ground under his feet, and knew from that, that he had at last come to some road. He tried now to follow this, for a road, he thought, was bound to lead to some place or other, but then the road ended at an open space in the forest, and there was neither road nor path, only drifts and loose snow. Then the old man's courage failed him; he felt like some poor creature destined to die a lonely death in the wilderness.

He began to grow tired of dragging himself through the snow, and, time after time, he sat down on a stone to rest, but as soon as he sat down, he felt he was on the point of falling asleep, and he knew he would be frozen to death if he did fall asleep; therefore, he tried to walk and walk— that was the only thing that could save him. But all at once, he could not resist the inclination to sit down. He thought if he could only rest, it did not matter if it did cost him his life.

It was so delightful to sit down that the thought of death did not in the least frighten him. He felt a kind of happiness at the thought that when he was dead the account of his whole life would be read aloud in church. He thought of how beautifully the old Dean had spoken about his father, and how something equally beautiful would be sure to be said about him. The Dean would say that he had owned the oldest farm in the district, and he would speak about the honor it was to belong to such a distinguished family, and then something would be said about responsibility. Of course, there was responsibility in the matter; that, he had always known. One must endure to the very last when one was an Ingmar.

The thought rushed through him that it was not befitting for him to be found frozen to death in the wild forest. He would not have that handed down to posterity, and he stood up again and began to walk. He had been sitting so long that masses of snow fell from his fur coat when he moved. But soon he sat down again and began to dream.

The thought of death now came quite gently to him. He thought about the whole of the funeral and all the honor they would show his dead body. He could see the table laid for the great funeral feast in the large room on the first floor—the Dean and his wife in the seats of honor; the Justice of the Peace, with the white frill spread over his narrow chest; the Major's wife in full dress, with a low silk bodice, and her neck covered with pearls and gold. He saw all the best rooms draped in white—white sheets before the windows, white over the furniture; branches of fir strewn the whole way from the entrance hall to the church; housecleaning and butchering, brewing and baking for a fortnight before the funeral; the corpse on a bier in the inmost room; smoke from the newly lighted fires in the rooms; the whole house crowded with guests; singing over the body whilst the lid of the coffin was being screwed on; silver plates on the coffin; twenty loads of wood burned in a fortnight; the whole village busy cooking food to take to the funeral; all the tall hats newly ironed; all the corn brandy from the autumn drunk up during the funeral feast; all the road crowded with people as at fair time.

Again the old man started up. He had heard them sitting and talking about him during the feast.

"But how did he manage to go and get frozen to death?" asked the Justice of the Peace. "What could he have been doing in the large forest?"

And the Captain would say that it was probably from Christmas ale and the corn brandy. And that roused him again. The Ingmars had never been drunkards. It should never be said of him that he was muddled in his last moments. And he began again to walk and walk, but he was so tired that he could scarcely stand on his legs. It was quite clear to him now that he had got far into the forest, for there were no paths anywhere, but many large rocks of which he knew there were none lower down. His foot caught between two stones, so that he had difficulty in getting it out, and he stood and moaned. He was quite done for.

Suddenly he fell over a heap of fagots. He fell softly onto the snow and branches, so he was not hurt, but he did not take the trouble to get up again. He had no other desire in the world than to sleep. He pushed the fagots to one side and crept under them as if they were a rug, but when he pushed himself under the branches, he felt that underneath there was something warm and soft. This must be a bear, he thought.

He felt the animal move, and heard it sniff, but he lay still. The bear might eat him if it liked, he thought. He had not strength enough to move a single step to get out of its way.

But it seemed as if the bear did not want to harm anyone who sought its protection on such a night as this. It moved a little further into its lair, as if to make room for its visitor, and directly afterward, it slept again with even, snorting breath.

In the meantime there was but scanty Christmas joy in the old farm of the Ingmars. The whole of Christmas Eve, they were looking for Ingmar Ingmarson. First, they went all over the dwelling house and all the outhouses. They searched high and low, from loft to cellar. Then they went to neighboring farms and inquired for Ingmar Ingmarson.

As they did not find him, his sons and his sons-in-law went into the fields and roads. They used the torches which should have lighted the way for people going to early service on Christmas morning in the search for him. The terrible snowstorm had hidden all traces, and the howling of the wind drowned the sound of their voices when they called and shouted. They were out and about until long after midnight, but then they saw that it was useless to continue the search, and that they must wait until daylight to find the old man.

At the first pale streak of dawn, everybody was up at Ingmar's farm, and the men stood about the yard ready to set out for the wood. But before they started, the old housewife came and called them into the best room. She told them to sit down on the long benches; she herself sat down by the Christmas table with the Bible in front of her and began to read. She tried her best to find something suitable for the occasion, and chose the story of the man who was traveling from Jerusalem to Jericho and fell among thieves.

She read slowly and monotonously about the unfortunate man who was succored by the good samaritan. Her sons and sons-in-law, her daughters and daughters-in-law, sat around her on the benches. They all resembled her and each other, big and clumsy, with plain, old-fashioned faces, for they all belonged to the old race of the Ingmars. They all had reddish hair, freckled skin, and light blue eyes with white eyelashes. They might be different enough from each other in some ways, but they all had a stern look about the mouth, dull eyes, and heavy movements, as if everything were a trouble to them. But one could see that they all, every one of them, belonged to the first people in the neighborhood, and that they knew themselves to be better than other people.

All the sons and daughters of the house of Ingmar sighed deeply during the reading of the Bible. They wondered if some good samaritan had found the master of the house and taken care of him, for all the Ingmars felt as if they had lost a part of their own soul when a misfortune happened to anyone belonging to the family.

The old woman read and read, and came to the question: "Who was neighbor unto him that fell amongst the thieves?" But before she had read the answer, the door opened and old Ingmar came into the room.

"Mother, here is Father," said one of the daughters, and the answer, that the man's neighbor was he who had shown mercy unto him, was never read.

Later in the day, the housewife sat again in the same place, and read her Bible. She was alone; the women had gone to church, and the men were bear-hunting in the forest. As soon as Ingmar Ingmarson had eaten and drunk, he took his sons with him and went out to the forest, for it is every man's duty to kill a bear wherever and whenever he comes across one. It does not do to spare a bear for, sooner or later, it will get a taste for flesh, and then it will spare neither man nor beast.

But after they were gone, a great feeling of fear came over the old housewife, and she began to read her Bible. She read the lesson for the day, which was also the text for the Pastor's sermon, but she did not get further than this: "Peace on earth, goodwill toward men." She remained sitting and staring at these words with her dull eyes, now and again sighing deeply. She did not read any further, but she repeated time after time in her slow, drawling voice, "Peace on earth, goodwill toward men."

The eldest son came into the room just as she was going to repeat the words afresh.

"Mother!" he said softly.

She heard him, but did not take her eyes from the book whilst she asked:

"Are you not with the others in the forest?"

"Yes," said he, still more softly, "I have been there."

123

"Come to the table," she said, "so that I can see you."

He came nearer, but when she looked at him, she saw that he was trembling. He had to press his hands hard against the edge of the table in order to keep them still.

"Have you got the bear?" she asked again.

He could not answer; he only shook his head.

The old woman got up and did what she had not done since her son was a child. She went up to him, laid her hand on his arm, and drew him to the bench. She sat down beside him and took his hand to hers.

"Tell me now what has happened, my boy."

The young man recognized the caress which had comforted him in bygone days when he had been in trouble and unhappy, and he was so overcome that he began to weep.

"I suppose it is something about Father?" she said.

"It is worse than that," the son sobbed.

"Worse than that?"

The young man cried more and more violently; he did not know how to control his voice. At last, he lifted his rough hand, with the broad fingers, and pointed to what she had just read: "Peace on earth..."

"Is it anything about that?" she asked.

"Yes," he answered.

"You wished to do an evil deed this morning?"

"Yes."

"And God has punished us?"

"God has punished us."

So at last she was told how it happened. They had, with some trouble, found the lair of the bear, and when they had got near enough to see the heap of fagots, they stopped in order to load their guns. But before they were ready, the bear rushed out of its lair straight against them. It went neither to the right nor to the left, but straight for old Ingmar Ingmarson, and struck him a blow on the top of the head that felled him to the ground, as if he had been struck by lightning. It did not attack any of

124

the others, but rushed past them into the forest.

In the afternoon Ingmar Ingmarson's wife and son drove to the Dean's house to announce his death. The son was spokesman, and the old housewife sat and listened with a face as immovable as a stone figure.

The Dean sat in his easy chair near his writing table. He had entered the death in the register. He had done it rather slowly; he wanted time to consider what he should say to the widow and the son, for this was, indeed, an unusual case. The son had told him frankly how it had all happened, but the Dean was anxious to know how they themselves looked at it. They were peculiar people, the Ingmars.

When the Dean had closed the book, the son said:

"We wanted to tell you, Sir, that we do not wish any account of Father's life be read in church."

The Dean pushed his spectacles over his forehead and looked searchingly at the old woman. She sat just as immovable as before. She only crumpled the handkerchief a little which she held in her hand.

"We wish to have him buried on a weekday," continued the son.

"Indeed!" said the Dean.

He could hardly believe his own ears. Old Ingmar Ingmarson to be buried without anyone taking notice of it—the congregation not to stand on railings and mounds in order to see the display as he was carried to the grave!

"There will not be any funeral feast. We have let the neighbors know that they need not think of preparing anything for the funeral."

"Indeed, indeed!" said the Dean again.

He could think of nothing else to say. He knew quite well what it meant for such people to forego the funeral feast. He had seen both widows and the fatherless comforted by giving a splendid funeral feast.

"There will be no funeral procession, only I and my brothers."

The Dean looked almost appealingly at the old woman. Could she really be a party to all of this? He asked himself if it could be her wishes to which the son had given expression. She was sitting there and allowing herself to be robbed of what must be dearer to her than gold and silver.

"We will not have the bells rung, or any silver plates on the coffin. Mother and I wish it to be done in this way, but we tell you all this, Sir, in order to hear, Sir, if you think we are wronging father."

Now the old woman spoke:

"We should like to hear if your Reverence thinks we are doing Father a wrong."

The Dean remained silent, and the old woman continued, more eagerly:

"I must tell your Reverence that if my husband had sinned against the king or the authorities, or if I had been obliged to cut him down from the gallows, he should all the same have had an honorable funeral, as his father before him, for the Ingmars are not afraid of anyone, and they need not go out of their way for anybody. But at Christmas, God made peace between man and beast, and the poor beast kept God's commandment whilst we broke it, and, therefore, we now suffer God's punishment, and it is not becoming for us to show any ostentatious display."

The Dean rose and went up to the old woman.

"What you say is right," he said, "and you shall follow the dictates of your own conscience." And involuntarily he added, perhaps most to himself: "The Ingmars are a grand family."

The old woman straightened herself a little at these words. At that moment, the Dean saw in her the symbol of her whole race. He understood what it was that had made these heavy, silent people, century after century, the leaders if the whole parish.

"It behooves the Ingmars to set the people a good example," she said. "It behooves us to show that we humble ourselves before God."

126

The Legend of the Christmas Rose

Robber Mother, who lived in Robbers' Cave up in Göinge forest, went down to the village one day on a begging tour. Robber Father, who was an outlawed man, did not dare to leave the forest, but had to content himself with lying in wait for the wayfarers who ventured within its borders. But at that time travelers were not very plentiful in southern Skåne. If it so happened that the man had had a few weeks of ill luck with his hunt, his wife would take to the road. She took with her five youngsters, and each youngster wore a ragged leathern suit and birchbark shoes and bore a sack on his back as long as himself. When Robber Mother stepped inside the door of a cabin, no one dared refuse to give her whatever she demanded; for she was not above coming back the following night and setting fire to the house if she had not been well received. Robber Mother and her brood were worse than a pack of wolves, and many a man felt like running a spear through them, but it was never done, because they all knew that the man stayed up in the forest, and he would have known how to wreak vengeance if anything had happened to the children or the old woman.

Now that Robber Mother went from house to house and begged, she came one day to Övid, which at that time was a cloister. She rang the bell of the cloister gate and asked for food. The watchman let down a small wicket in the gate and handed her six round bread cakes—one for herself and one for each of the five children.

While the mother was standing quietly at the gate, her youngsters were running about. And now one of them came and pulled at her skirt, as a signal that he had discovered something which she ought to come and see, and

Robber Mother followed him promptly.

The entire cloister was surrounded by a high and strong wall, but the youngster had managed to find a little back gate which stood ajar. When Robber Mother got there, she pushed the gate open and walked inside without asking leave, as it was her custom to do.

Övid Cloister was managed at that time by Abbot Hans, who knew all about herbs. Just within the cloister wall he had planted a little herb garden, and it was into this that the old woman had forced her way.

At first glance, Robber Mother was so astonished that she paused at the gate. It was high summertide, and Abbot Hans's garden was so full of flowers that the eyes were fairly dazzled by the blues, reds, and yellows, as one looked into it. But presently an indulgent smile spread over her features, and she started to walk up a narrow path that lay between many flower beds.

In the garden, a lay brother walked about, pulling up weeds. It was he who had left the door in the wall open, that he might throw the weeds and tares on the rubbish heap outside.

When he saw Robber Mother coming in, with all five youngsters in tow, he ran toward her at once and ordered them away. But the beggar woman walked right on as before. She cast her eyes up and down, looking now at the stiff white lilies which spread near the ground, then on the ivy climbing high upon the cloister wall, and took no notice whatever of the lay brother.

He thought she had not understood him, and wanted to take her by the arm and turn her toward the gate, but when the robber woman saw his purpose, she gave him a look that sent him reeling backward. She had been walking with back bent under her beggar's pack, but now she straightened to her full height. "I am Robber Mother from Göinge forest, so touch me if you dare!" It was obvious that she was as certain she would be left in peace as if she had announced that she was the Queen of Denmark.

And yet the lay brother dared to oppose her, although now, when he knew who she was, he spoke reasonably to her. "You must know, Robber Mother, that this is a monks' cloister, and no woman in the land is allowed within these walls. If you do not go away, the monks will be angry with me because I forgot to close the gate, and perhaps they will drive me away from the cloister and the herb garden."

But such prayers were wasted on Robber Mother. She walked straight ahead among the little flower beds and looked at the hyssop with its magenta blossoms, and at the honeysuckles, which were full of deep orange-colored flower clusters.

Then the lay brother knew of no other remedy than to run into the cloister and call for help.

He returned with two stalwart monks, and Robber Mother saw that now it meant business! With feet firmly planted she stood in the path and began shrieking in strident tones all the awful vengeance she would wreak on the cloister if she couldn't remain in the herb garden as long as she wished. But the monks did not see why they need fear her and thought only of driving her out. Then Robber Mother let out a perfect volley of shrieks, and, throwing herself upon the monks, clawed and bit at them; so did all the youngsters. The men soon learned that she could overpower them, and all they could do was to go back into the cloister for reinforcements.

As they ran through the passageway which led to the cloister, they met Abbot Hans, who came rushing out to learn what all this noise was about.

Then they had to confess that Robber Mother from Göinge forest had come into the cloister and that they were unable to drive her out and must call for assistance.

But Abbot Hans upbraided them for using force and forbade their calling for help. He sent both monks back to their work, and although he was an old and fragile man, he took with him only the lay brother.

When Abbot Hans came out in the garden, Robber

129

Mother was still wandering among the flower beds. He regarded her with astonishment. He was certain that Robber Mother had never before seen an herb garden; yet she sauntered leisurely between all the small patches, each of which had been planted with its own species of rare flower, and looked at them as if they were old acquaintances. At some she smiled; at others she shook her head.

Abbot Hans loved his herb garden as much as it was possible for him to love anything earthly and perishable. Wild and terrible as the old woman looked, he couldn't help liking that she had fought with three monks for the privilege of viewing the garden in peace. He came up to her and asked in a mild tone if the garden pleased her.

Robber Mother turned defiantly toward Abbot Hans, for she expected only to be trapped and overpowered. But when she noticed his white hair and bent form, she answered peaceably, "First, when I saw this, I thought I had never seen a prettier garden, but now I see that it can't be compared with one I know of."

Abbot Hans had certainly expected a different answer. When he heard that Robber Mother had seen a garden more beautiful than his, a faint flush spread over his withered cheek. The lay brother, who was standing close by, immediately began to censure the old woman. "This is Abbot Hans," said he, "who with much care and diligence has gathered the flowers from far and near for his herb garden. We all know that there is not a more beautiful garden to be found in all Skåne, and it is not befitting that you, who live in the wild forest all the year around, should find fault with his work."

"I don't wish to make myself the judge of either him or you," said Robber Mother. "I'm only saying that if you could see the garden of which I am thinking, you would uproot all the flowers planted here and cast them away like weeds."

But the Abbot's assistant was hardly less proud of the

flowers than the Abbot himself, and after hearing her remarks, he laughed derisively. "I can understand that you only talk like this to tease us. It must be a pretty garden that you have made for yourself amongst the pines in Göinge forest! I'd be willing to wager my soul's salvation that you have never before been within the walls of an herb garden."

Robber Mother grew crimson with rage to think that her word was doubted, and she cried out: "It may be true that until today I had never been within the walls of an herb garden, but you monks, who are holy men, certainly must know that on every Christmas Eve the great Göinge forest is transformed into a beautiful garden to commemorate the hour of our Lord's birth. We who live in the forest have seen this happen every year. And in that garden, I have seen flowers so lovely that I dared not lift my hand to pluck them."

The lay brother wanted to continue the argument, but Abbot Hans gave him a sign to be silent. For, ever since his childhood, Abbot Hans had heard it said that on every Christmas Eve the forest was dressed in holiday glory. He had often longed to see it, but he had never had the good fortune. Eagerly, he begged and implored Robber Mother that he might come up to the Robbers' Cave on Christmas Eve. If she would only send one of her children to show him the way, he could ride up there alone, and he would never betray them—on the contrary, he would reward them, in so far as it lay in his power.

Robber Mother said no at first, for she was thinking of Robber Father and of the peril which might befall him should she permit Abbot Hans to ride up to their cave. At the same time, the desire to prove to the monk that the garden which she knew was more beautiful than his got the better of her, and she gave in.

"But more than one follower you cannot take with you," said she, "and you are not to waylay us or trap us, as sure as you are a holy man."

This Abbot Hans promised, and then Robber Mother went her way. Abbot Hans commanded the lay brother not to reveal to a soul that which had been agreed upon. He feared that the monks, should they learn of his purpose, would not allow a man of his years to go up to the Robbers' Cave.

Nor did he himself intend to reveal his project to a single human being. And then it happened that Archbishop Absalon from Lund came to Övid and remained through the night. When Abbot Hans was showing him the herb garden, he got to thinking of Robber Mother's visit, and the lay brother, who was at work in the garden, heard Abbot Hans telling the bishop about Robber Father, who these many years had lived as an outlaw in the forest, and asking him for a letter of ransom for the man, that he might lead an honest life among respectable folk. "As things are now," said Abbot Hans, "his children are growing up into worse malefactors than himself, and you will soon have a whole gang of robbers to deal with up there in the forest."

But the Archbishop replied that he did not care to let the robber loose among honest folk in the villages. It would be best for all that he remain in the forest.

Then Abbot Hans grew zealous and told the bishop all about Göinge forest, which, every year at Yuletide, clothed itself in summer bloom around the Robbers' Cave. "If these bandits are not so bad but that God's glories can be made manifest to them, surely we cannot be too wicked to experience the same blessing."

The Archbishop knew how to answer Abbot Hans. "This much I will promise you, Abbot Hans," he said, smiling, "that any day you send me a blossom from the garden in Göinge forest, I will give you letters of ransom for all the outlaws you may choose to plead for."

The lay brother apprehended that Bishop Absalon believed as little in this story of Robber Mother's as he himself, but Abbot Hans perceived nothing of the sort, and thanked Absalon for his good promise, and said that he would surely send him the flower.

Abbot Hans had his way. The following Christmas Eve he did not sit at home with his monks in Övid Cloister, but was on his way to Göinge forest. One of Robber Mother's wild youngsters ran ahead of him, and close behind him was the lay brother who had talked with Robber Mother in the herb garden.

Abbot Hans had been longing to make this journey, and he was very happy now that it had come to pass. But it was a different matter with the lay brother who accompanied him. Abbot Hans was very dear to him, and he would not willingly have allowed another to attend him and watch over him; but he didn't believe that he should see any Christmas Eve garden. He thought the whole thing a snare which Robber Mother had, with great cunning, laid for Abbot Hans, that he might fall into her husband's clutches.

While Abbot Hans was riding toward the forest, he saw that everywhere they were preparing to celebrate Christmas. In every peasant settlement, fires were lighted in the bathhouse to warm it for the afternoon bathing. Great hunks of meat and bread were being carried from the larders into the cabins, and from the barns came the men with big sheaves of straw to be strewn over the floors.

As he rode by the little country churches, he observed that each parson, with his sexton, was busily engaged in decorating his church, and when he came to the road which leads to Bösjo Cloister, he observed that all the poor of the parish were coming with armfuls of bread and long candles, which they had received at the cloister gate.

When Abbot Hans saw all these Christmas preparations, his haste increased. He was thinking of the festivities that awaited him, which were greater than any the others would be privileged to enjoy.

But the lay brother whined and fretted when he saw how they were preparing to celebrate Christmas in every

133

humble cottage. He grew more and more anxious, and begged and implored Abbot Hans to turn back and not to throw himself deliberately into the robber's hands.

Abbot Hans went straight ahead, paying no heed to his lamentations. He left the plain behind him and came up into desolate and wild forest regions. Here the road was bad, almost like a stony and burr-strewn path, with neither bridge nor plank to help them over brooklet and rivulet. The farther they rode, the colder it grew, and after a while they came upon snow-covered ground.

It turned out to be a long and hazardous ride through the forest. They climbed steep and slippery side paths, crawled over swamp and marsh, and pushed through windfall and bramble. Just as daylight was waning, the robber boy guided them across a forest meadow, skirted by tall, naked leaf trees and green fir trees. Back of the meadow loomed a mountain wall, and in this wall they saw a door of thick boards. Now Abbot Hans understood that they had arrived, and dismounted. The child opened the heavy door for him, and he looked into a poor mountain grotto with bare stone walls. Robber Mother was seated before a log fire that burned in the middle of the floor. Alongside the walls were beds of virgin pine and moss, and on one of these beds lay Robber Father asleep.

"Come in, you out there!" shouted Robber Mother without rising, "and fetch the horses in with you, so they won't be destroyed by the night cold."

Abbot Hans walked boldly into the cave, and the lay brother followed. Here were wretchedness and poverty, and nothing was being done to celebrate Christmas. Robber Mother had neither brewed nor baked; she had neither washed nor scoured. The youngsters were lying on the floor around a kettle, eating, but no better food was provided for them than a watery gruel.

Robber Mother spoke in a tone as haughty and dictatorial as any well-to-do peasant woman. "Sit down by the fire and warm yourself, Abbot Hans," said she, "and if you have food with you, eat, for the food which we in the forest prepare, you wouldn't care to taste. And if you are tired after the long journey, you can lie down on one of these beds to sleep. You needn't be afraid of oversleeping, for I'm sitting here by the fire keeping watch. I shall awaken you in time to see that which you have come up here to see."

Abbot Hans obeyed Robber Mother and brought forth his food sack, but he was so fatigued after the journey, he was hardly able to eat, and as soon as he could stretch himself on the bed, he fell asleep.

The lay brother was also assigned a bed to rest upon, but he didn't dare sleep, as he thought he had better keep his eye on Robber Father to prevent his getting up and capturing Abbot Hans. But gradually fatigue got the better of him, too, and he dropped into a doze.

When he woke up, he saw that Abbot Hans had left his bed and was sitting by the fire talking with Robber Mother. The outlawed robber sat also by the fire. He was a tall, raw-boned man with a dull, sluggish appearance. His back was turned to Abbot Hans, as though he would have it appear that he was not listening to the conversation.

Abbot Hans was telling Robber Mother all about the Christmas preparations he had seen on the journey, reminding her of Christmas feasts and games which she must have known in her youth when she lived at peace with mankind. "I'm sorry for your children, who can never run on the village street in holiday dress or tumble in the Christmas straw," said he.

At first Robber Mother answered in short, gruff sentences, but by degrees she became more subdued and listened more intently. Suddenly Robber Father turned toward Abbot Hans and shook his clenched fist in his face. "You miserable monk! Did you come here to coax from me my wife and children? Don't you know that I am an outlaw and may not leave the forest?"

Abbot Hans looked him fearlessly in the eyes. "It is my

purpose to get a letter of ransom for you from Archbishop Absalon," said he. He had hardly finished speaking when the robber and his wife burst out laughing. They knew well enough the kind of mercy a forest robber could expect from Bishop Absalon!

"Oh, if I get a letter of ransom from Absalon," said Robber Father, "then I'll promise you that never again will I steal so much as a goose."

The lay brother was annoyed with the robber folk for daring to laugh at Abbot Hans, but on his own account he was well pleased. He had seldom seen the abbot sitting more peaceful and meek with his monks at Övid than he now sat with this wild robber folk.

Suddenly Robber Mother rose. "As you sit here and talk, Abbot Hans," she said, "we are forgetting to look at the forest. Now I can hear, even in this cave, how the Christmas bells are ringing."

The words were barely uttered when they all sprang up and rushed out. But in the forest it was still dark night and bleak winter. The only thing they marked was a distant clang borne on a light south wind.

"How can this bell ringing ever awaken the dead forest?" thought Abbot Hans. For now, as he stood out in the winter darkness, he thought it far more impossible that a summer garden could spring up here than it had seemed to him before.

When the bells had been ringing a few moments, a sudden illumination penetrated the forest; the next moment it was dark again, and then the light came back. It pushed its way forward between the stark trees, like a shimmering mist. This much it effected: the darkness merged into a faint daybreak. Then Abbot Hans saw that the snow had vanished from the ground, as if someone had removed a carpet, and the earth began to take on a green covering. Then the ferns shot up their fronds, rolled like a bishop's staff. Heather grew on the stony hills and the bog-myrtle rooted in the ground moss dressed themselves quickly in new bloom. Moss tufts thickened and raised themselves, and spring blossoms shot upward their swelling buds, which already had a touch of color.

Abbot Hans's heart beat fast as he marked the first signs of the forest's awakening. "Old man that I am, shall I behold such a miracle?" thought he, and the tears wanted to spring to his eyes. Again it grew so hazy that he feared the darkness would once more cover the earth, but almost immediately there came a new wave of light. It brought with it the splash of rivulet and the rush of cataract. Then the leaves of the trees burst into bloom, as if a swarm of green butterflies came flying and clustered on the branches. It was not only trees and plants that awoke, but crossbeaks hopped from branch to branch, and woodpeckers hammered on the limbs until the splinters fairly flew around them. A flock of starlings from up country lighted in a fir top to rest. They were paradise starlings. The tips of each tiny feather shone in brilliant reds, and, as the birds moved, they glittered like so many jewels.

Again, all was dark for an instant, but soon there came a new light wave. A fresh, warm south wind blew and scattered over the forest meadow all the little seeds that had been brought here from southern lands by birds and ships and winds, and which could not thrive elsewhere because of this country's cruel cold. These took root and sprang up the instant they touched the ground.

When the next warm wind came along, the blueberries and lingon ripened. Cranes and wild geese shrieked in the air; the bullfinches built nests, and baby squirrels began playing on the branches of the trees.

Everything came so fast now that Abbot Hans could not stop to reflect on how immeasurably great was the miracle that was taking place. He had time only to use his eyes and ears. The next light wave that came rushing in brought with it the scent of newly ploughed acres, and far off in the distance, milkmaids were heard coaxing the cows—and the tinkle of the sheep's bells. Pine and spruce trees were so thickly clothed with red cones that they shone like crimson mantles. The juniper berries changed color every second, and forest flowers covered the ground till it was all red, blue, and yellow.

Abbot Hans bent down to the earth and broke off a wild strawberry blossom, and, as he straightened up, the berry ripened in his hand.

A mother fox came out of her lair with a big litter of black-legged young. She went up to Robber Mother and scratched at her skirt, and Robber Mother bent down to her and praised her young. The horned owl, who had just begun his night chase, was astonished at the light and went back to his ravine to perch for the night. The male cuckoo crowed, and his mate stole up to the nests of the little birds with her egg in her mouth.

Robber Mother's youngsters let out perfect shrieks of delight. They stuffed themselves with wild strawberries, large as pine cones, that hung on the bushes. One of them played with a litter of young hares; another ran a race with some young crows, which had hopped from their nest before they were really ready; a third caught up an adder from the ground and wound it around his neck and arm.

Robber Father was standing out on a marsh eating raspberries. When he glanced up, a big black bear stood beside him. Robber Father broke off an osier twig and struck the bear on the nose. "Keep to your own ground, you!" he said. "This is my turf." Then the huge bear turned around and lumbered off in another direction.

New waves of warmth and light kept coming, and now they brought with them seeds from the star-flower. Golden pollen from rye fields fairly flew in the air. Then came butterflies, so big that they looked like flying lilies. The beehive in a hollow oak was already so full of honey that it dripped down on the trunk of the tree. Then all the flowers whose seeds had been brought from foreign lands began to blossom. The loveliest roses climbed up the mountain wall in a race with the blackberry vines, and from the forest meadow sprang flowers as large as human faces.

Abbot Hans thought of the flower he was to pluck for Bishop Absalon, but each new flower that appeared was more beautiful than the others, and he wanted to choose the most beautiful of all.

Wave upon wave kept coming until the air was so filled with light that it glittered. All the life and beauty and joy of summer smiled on Abbot Hans. He felt that earth could bring no greater happiness than that which welled up about him, and he said to himself, "I do not know what new beauties the next wave that comes can bring with it."

But the light kept streaming in, and now it seemed to Abbot Hans that it carried with it something from an infinite distance. He felt a celestial atmosphere enfolding him, and tremblingly he began to anticipate, now that earth's joys had come, that the glories of heaven were approaching.

Then Abbot Hans marked how all grew still: the birds hushed their songs; the flowers ceased growing, and the young foxes played no more. The glory now nearing was such that the heart wanted to stop beating; the eyes wept without one's knowing it; the soul longed to soar away into the Eternal. From far in the distance, faint harp tones were heard, and celestial song, like a soft murmur, reached him.

Abbot Hans clasped his hands and dropped to his knees. His face was radiant with bliss. Never had he dreamed that, even in this life, it should be granted him to taste the joys of heaven, and to hear angels sing Christmas carols!

But beside Abbot Hans stood the lay brother who had accompanied him. In his mind there were dark thoughts. "This cannot be a true miracle," he thought, "since it is revealed to malefactors. This does not come from God, but has its origin in witchcraft and is sent hither by Satan. It is the Evil One's power that is tempting us and compelling us to see that which has no real existence."

From afar were heard the sound of angel harps and the tones of a "Miserere." But the lay brother thought it was the evil spirits of hell coming closer. "They would enchant and seduce us," sighed he, "and we shall be sold into perdition."

The angel throng was so near now that Abbot Hans saw their bright forms through the forest branches. The lay brother saw them, too, but back of all this wondrous beauty he saw only some dread evil. For him it was the devil who performed these wonders on the anniversary of our Saviour's birth. It was done simply for the purpose of more effectually deluding poor human beings.

All the while, the birds had been circling around the head of Abbot Hans, and they let him take them in his hands. But all the animals were afraid of the lay brother: no bird perched on his shoulder; no snake played at his feet. Then came a little forest dove. When she marked that the angels were nearing, she plucked up courage and flew down on the lay brother's shoulder and laid her head against his cheek.

Then it appeared to him as if sorcery were come right upon him to tempt and corrupt him. He struck with his hand at the forest dove and cried in such a loud voice that it rang throughout the forest, "Go thou back to hell, whence thou art come!"

Just then the angels were so near that Abbot Hans felt the feathery touch of their great wings, and he bowed down to earth in reverent greeting.

But when the lay brother's words sounded, their song was hushed and the holy guests turned in flight. At the same time, the light and the mild warmth vanished in unspeakable terror for the darkness and cold in a human heart. Darkness sank over the earth like a coverlet; frost came; all the growths shrivelled up; the animals and birds hastened away; the rushing of streams was hushed; the leaves dropped from the trees, rustling like rain.

Abbot Hans felt how his heart, which had but lately swelled with bliss, was now contracting with insufferable agony. "I can never outlive this," thought he, "that the angels from heaven had been so close to me and were driven away; that they wanted to sing Christmas carols for me and were driven to flight."

Then he remembered the flower he had promised Bishop Absalon, and at the last moment, he fumbled among the leaves and moss to try and find a blossom. But he sensed how the ground under his fingers froze and how the white snow came gliding over the ground. Then his heart caused him ever greater anguish. He could not rise, but fell prostrate on the ground and lay there.

When the robber folk and the lay brother had groped their way back to the cave, they missed Abbot Hans. They took brands with them and went out to search for him. They found him dead upon the coverlet of snow.

Then the lay brother began weeping and lamenting, for he understood that it was he who had killed Abbot Hans, because he had dashed from him the cup of happiness which he had been thirsting to drain to its last drop.

When Abbot Hans had been carried down to Övid, those who took charge of the dead saw that he held his right hand locked tight around something which he must have grasped at the moment of death. When they finally got his hand open, they found that the thing which he had held in such an iron grip was a pair of white root bulbs, which he had torn from among the moss and leaves.

When the lay brother who had accompanied Abbot Hans saw the bulbs, he took them and planted them in Abbot Hans' herb garden.

He guarded them the whole year to see if any flower would spring from them. But in vain he waited through the spring, the summer, and the autumn. Finally, when winter had set in and all the leaves and the flowers were dead, he ceased caring for them.

But when Christmas Eve came again, he was so strongly reminded of Abbot Hans that he wandered out into the garden to think of him. And look! as he came to the spot where he had planted the bare root bulbs, he saw that from them had sprung flourishing green stalks, which bore beautiful flowers with silver white leaves.

He called out all the monks at Övid, and when they saw that this plant bloomed on Christmas Eve, when all the other growths were as if dead, they understood that this flower had in truth been plucked by Abbot Hans from the Christmas garden in Göinge forest. Then the lay brother asked the monks if he might take a few blossoms to Bishop Absalon.

And when he appeared before Bishop Absalon, he gave him the flowers and said: "Abbot Hans sends you these. They are the flowers he promised to pick for you from the garden in Göinge forest."

When Bishop Absalon beheld the flowers, which had sprung from the earth in darkest winter, and heard the words, he turned as pale as if he had met a ghost. He sat in silence a moment; thereupon he said, "Abbot Hans has faithfully kept his word, and I shall also keep mine." And he ordered that a letter of ransom be drawn up for the wild robber who was outlawed, and had been forced to live in the forest ever since his youth.

He handed the letter to the lay brother, who departed at once for the Robbers' Cave. When he stepped in there on Christmas Day, the robber came toward him with axe uplifted. "I'd like to hack you monks into bits, as many as you are!" said he. "It must be your fault that Göinge forest did not last night dress itself in Christmas bloom."

"The fault is mine alone," said the lay brother, "and I will gladly die for it, but first I must deliver a message from Abbot Hans." And he drew forth the bishop's letter and told the man that he was free. "Hereafter you and your children shall play in the Christmas straw and celebrate your Christmas among people, just as Abbot Hans wished to have it," said he.

Then Robber Father stood there pale and speechless, but Robber Mother said in his name, "Abbot Hans has indeed kept his word, and Robber Father will keep his."

When the robber and his wife left the cave, the lay brother moved in and lived all alone in the forest, in constant meditation and prayer that his hard-heartedness might be forgiven him.

But Göinge forest never again celebrated the hour of our Saviour's birth, and of all its glory, there lives today only the plant which Abbot Hans had plucked. It has been named Christmas Rose. And each year at Christmastide, she sends forth from the earth her green stalks and white blossoms, as if she never could forget that she had once grown in the great Christmas garden at Göinge forest.

The Brothers

It is very possible that I am mistaken, but it seems that an astonishing number of people are dying this year. I have a feeling that I cannot go down the street without meeting a hearse. One cannot help thinking about all those who are carried to the churchyard. I always feel as if it were so sad for the dead who have to be buried in towns. I can hear how they moan in their coffins. Some complain that they have not had plumes on the hearse; some count up the wreaths, and are not satisfied, and then there are some who have only been followed by two or three carriages, and who are hurt by that.

The dead ought never to know and experience such things, but people in towns do not understand how they ought to honor those who have entered into eternal rest.

When I really think it over, I do not know any place where they understand death better than at home in Svartsjö. If you die in the parish of Svartsjö, you know you will have a coffin like that of everyone else—an honest black coffin which is like the coffins in which the country judge and local magistrate were buried a year or two ago. For the same joiner makes all the coffins, and he has only one pattern; the one is made neither better nor worse than the other. And you know also, for you have seen it so many times, that you will be carried to the church on a wagon which has been painted black for the occasion. You need not trouble yourself at all about any plumes. And you know that the whole village will follow you to the church, and that they will drive as slowly and as solemnly for you as for a landed proprietor.

You will have no occasion to feel annoyed because you have not enough wreaths, for they do not place a single flower on the coffin; it shall stand out black and shining, and nothing must cover it, and it is not necessary for you to think whether you will have a sufficiently large number of people to follow you, for those who live in your town will be sure to follow you, every one. Nor will you be obliged to lie and listen if there is lamenting and weeping around your coffin. They never weep over the dead when they stand on the church hill outside Svartsjö Church. No, they weep as little over a strong young fellow, who falls a prey to death just as he is beginning to provide for his old people, as they will for you. You will be placed on a couple of black trestles outside the door of the parish room, and a whole crowd of people will gradually gather round you, and all the women will have handkerchiefs in their hands. But no one will cry; all the handkerchiefs will be kept tightly rolled up; not one will be applied to the eyes. You need not speculate as to whether people will shed as many tears over you as they would over others. They would cry if it were the proper thing, but it is not the proper thing.

You can understand that if there were much sorrowing over one grave, it would not look well for those over whom no one sorrowed. They know what they are about at Svartsjö. They do as it has been the custom to do there for many hundred years. But whilst you rest there, on the church hill, you are a great and important personage, although you receive neither flowers nor tears. No one comes to church without asking who you are, and then they go quietly up to you and stand and gaze at you, and it never occurs to anyone to wound the dead by pitying him. No one says anything but that it is well for him that it is all over.

It is not at all as it is in a town, where you can be buried any day. At Svartsjö you must be buried on a Sunday, so that you can have the whole parish around you. There you will have standing near your coffin both the girl with whom you danced at the last midsummer night's festival and the man with whom you exchanged horses at the last fair. You will have the schoolmaster who

145

took so much trouble with you when you were a little lad, and who had forgotten you, although you remembered him so well, and you will have the old member of Parliament who never before thought it worth his while to bow to you. This is not as in a town, where people hardly turn around when you are carried past. When they bring the long bands and place them under the coffin, there is not one who does not watch the proceedings.

You cannot imagine what a churchwarden we have at Svartsjö. He is an old soldier, and he looks like a field marshal. He has short white hair and twisted mustaches, and a pointed imperial; he is slim and tall and straight with a light and firm step. On Sundays he wears a well-brushed frock coat of fine cloth. He really looks a very fine old gentleman, and it is he who walks at the head of the procession. Then comes the verger—not that the verger is to be compared with the church warden. It is more than probable that his Sunday hat is too large and old-fashioned; as likely as not, he is awkward—but when is a verger not awkward?

Then you come next in your coffin with the six bearers, and then follow the clergyman and the clerk and the Town Council and the whole parish. All the congregation will follow you to the churchyard, you may be sure of that. But I will tell you something; all those who follow you look so small and poor. They are not fine townspeople, you know —only plain, simple Svartsjö folk. There is only one who is great and important, and that is you in your coffin—you who are dead.

The others, the next day, will have to resume their heavy and toilsome work. They will have to live in poor, old cottages and wear old, patched clothes; the others will always be plagued and worried, and dragged down and humbled by poverty.

Those who follow you to your grave become far more sad by looking at the living than by thinking of you who are dead. You need not look any more at the velvet collar of your coat to see if it is not getting worn at the edges; you need not make a special fold of your silk handkerchief to hide that it is beginning to fray; you will never more be compelled to ask the village shopkeeper to let you have goods on credit; you will not find out that your strength is failing; you will not have to wait for the day when you must go on the parish.

While they are following you to the grave, everyone will be thinking that it is best to be dead—better to soar heavenward, carried on the white clouds of the morning—than to be always experiencing life's manifold troubles. When they come to the wall of the churchyard, where the grave has been made, the bands are exchanged for strong ropes, and people get onto the loose earth and lower you down. And when this has been done, the clerk advances to the grave and begins to sing: "I walk towards death."

He sings the hymn quite alone: neither the clergyman nor any of the congregation help him. But the clerk must sing; however keen the north wind and however glaring the sun which shines straight in his face, sing he does.

The clerk, however, is getting old now, and he has not much voice left; he is quite aware that it does not sound as well now as formerly when he sang people into their graves, but he does it all the same—it is part of his duty. For the day, you understand, when his voice quite fails him so that he cannot sing anymore, he must resign his office, and this means downright poverty for him. Therefore the whole gathering stands in apprehension while the old clerk sings, wondering whether his voice will last through the whole verse. But no one joins him, not a single person, for that would not do; it is not the custom. People never sing at a grave at Svartsjö. People do not sing in the church either, except the first hymn on Christmas Day morning.

Still, if one listened very attentively, one could hear that the clerk does not sing alone. There is another voice, but it sounds so exactly the same that the two voices blend as if they were only one. The other who sings is a little old man in a long, coarse gray coat. He is still older than the clerk, but he gives out all the voice he has to help him. And the voice, as I have told you, is exactly the same kind as the clerk's; they are so alike one cannot help wondering at it.

But when one looks closer, the little, gray, old man is exactly like the clerk; he has the same nose and chin and mouth, only somewhat older, and, as it were, more hardly dealt with in life. And then one understands that the little, gray man is the clerk's brother, and then one knows why he helps him. For, you see, things have never gone well with him in this world, and he has always had bad luck, and once he was made a bankrupt and brought the clerk into his misfortunes. He knows that it is his fault that his brother has always had to struggle. And the clerk, you know, has tried to help him onto his legs again, but with no avail, for he has not been one of those one can help. He has always been unfortunate, and then, he has had no strength of purpose.

But the clerk has been the shining light in the family, and for the other, it has been a case of receiving and receiving, and he has never been able to make any return at all. Great God! Even to talk of making any return—he who is so poor! You only should see the little hut in the forest where he lives. He knows that he has always been dull and sad, only a burden—only a burden for his brother and for others. But now of late, he has become a great man; now he is able to give some return, and that he does. Now he helps his brother, the clerk, who has been the sunshine and life and joy for him all his days. Now he helps him to sing so that he may keep his office.

He does not go to church for he thinks that everyone looks at him because he has no black Sunday clothes, but every Sunday he goes to the church to see whether there is a coffin on the black trestles outside the parish room. If there is one, he goes to the grave in spite of his old, gray

148

coat, and helps his brother with his pitiful old voice.

The little old man knows very well how badly he sings; he places himself behind the others, and does not push forward to the grave. But sing he does; it would not matter so much if the clerk's voice should fail on one or another note; his brother is there and helps him.

At the churchyard, no one laughs at the singing, but when people go home and have thrown off their devoutness, then they speak of the service, and then they laugh at the clerk's singing—laugh both at his and his brother's. The clerk does not mind it; it is the same to him, but his brother thinks about it and suffers from it; he dreads the Sunday the whole week, but still he comes punctually to the churchyard and does his duty. But you in your coffin, you do not think so badly of the singing. You think that it is good music. Is it not true that one would like to be buried in Svartsjö if only for the sake of that singing?

It says in the hymn that life is but a walk towards death, and when the two old men sing this—the two who have suffered for each other during their whole life—then one understands better than ever before how wearisome it is to live, and one is so entirely satisfied with being dead.

And then the singing stops, and the clergyman throws earth on the coffin and says a prayer over you. Then the two old voices sing: "I walk towards heaven." And they do not sing this verse any better than the former; their voices grow more feeble and querulous the longer they sing. But for you a great and wide expanse opens, and you soar upward with tremulous joy, and everything earthly fades and disappears.

But still the last which you hear of things earthly tells of faithfulness and love. And in the midst of your trembling flight the poor song will awake memories of all the faithfulness and love you have met with here below, and this will bear you upward. This will fill you with radiance and make you beautiful as an angel.

The Story of a Story

Once there was a story that wanted to be told and sent out in the world. This was very natural, inasmuch as it knew that it was already as good as finished. Many, through remarkable deeds and strange events, had helped create it; others had added their straws in it by again and again relating these things. What it lacked was merely a matter of being joined together, so that it could travel comfortably through the country. As yet, it was only a confused jumble of stories—a big, formless cloud of adventures rushing hither and thither like a swarm of stray bees on a summer's day, not knowing where they will find someone who can gather them into a hive.

The story that wanted to be told had sprung up in Värmland, and you may be sure that it circled over many mills and manors, over many parsonages and many homes of military officers in the beautiful province, peering through the windows and begging to be cared for. But it was forced to make many futile attempts, for everywhere it was turned away. Anything else was hardly to be expected. People had many things of much more importance to think of.

Finally the story came to an old place called Mårbacka. It was a little homestead with low buildings overshadowed by giant trees. At one time, it had been a parsonage, and it was as if this had set a certain stamp upon the place which it could not lose. They seemed to have a greater love for books and reading there than elsewhere, and a certain air of restfulness and peace always pervaded it. There, rushing with duties and bickering with servants were never met with, nor was hatred or dissension given house room, either. One who happened to be a guest there was not allowed to take life too seriously, but had to feel that

150

his first duty was to be lighthearted and believe that for one and all who lived on this estate our Lord managed everything for the best.

As I think of the matter now, I apprehend that the story of which I am speaking must have lingered thereabouts a great many years during its vain longing to be told. It seems to me as though it must have enwrapped the place, as a mist shrouds a mountain summit, now and then letting one of the adventures of which it consisted rain down upon it.

They came in the form of strange ghost stories about the superintendent of the foundries, who always had black bulls hitched to his wagon when he drove home at night from a revel. And in his home, the Evil One himself used to sit in the rocker and rock while the wife sat at the piano and played. They came as true stories from the neighboring homestead, where crows had persecuted the mistress until she didn't dare venture outside the door; from the Captain's house, where they were so poor that everything had to be borrowed; from the little cottage down by the church, where there lived a lot of young and old girls who had all fallen in love with the handsome organ builder.

Sometimes the dear adventures came to the homestead in an even more tangible form. Aged and poverty-stricken army officers would drive up to the doorstep behind rickety old horses and in rickety carryalls. They would stop and visit for weeks, and in the evenings, when the toddy had put courage into them, they would talk of the time when they had danced in stockingless shoes so that their feet would look small, of how they had curled their hair and dyed their mustaches. One of them told how he had tried to take a pretty young girl back to her sweetheart and how he had been hunted by wolves on the way; another had been at the Christmas feast where an angered guest had flung all the hazel hens at the wall because someone had made him believe they were crows; a third had seen the old gentleman who used to sit at a plain board table and play Beethoven.

But the story could reveal its presence in still another way. In the attic hung the portrait of a lady with powdered hair, and when anyone walked past it, he was reminded that it was a portrait of the beautiful daughter of the count, who had loved her brother's young tutor, and had called to see him once when she was an old grayhaired lady and he an old married man. In the lumber room were heaped up bundles of documents containing deeds of purchase and leases signed by the great lady, who once ruled over seven foundries which had been willed to her by her lover. If one entered the church, one saw in a dusty little cabinet under the pulpit the chest filled with infidel manuscripts which was not to be opened until the beginning of the new century. And not very far from the church is the river, at the bottom of which rests a pile of sacred images that were not allowed to remain in the pulpit and chancel they once had ornamented.

It must have been because so many legends and traditions hovered around the farm that one of the children growing up there longed to become a narrator. It was not one of the boys. They were not at home very much, for they were away at their schools almost the whole year, so the story did not get much of a hold upon them. But it was one of the girls—one who was delicate and could not romp and play like other children, but found her greatest enjoyment in reading and hearing stories about all the great and wonderful things which had happened in the world.

At the start, it was not the girl's intention to write about the stories and legends surrounding her. She had not the remotest idea that a book could be made of these adventures, which she had so often heard related, that they seemed the most commonplace things in the world. When she tried to write, she chose material from books, and with fresh courage she strung together stories of the sultans in "Thousand and One Nights," Walter Scott's heroes, and Snorre Sturlason's "Kings of Romance."

Surely, it is needless to state that what she wrote was the least original and the crudest that has ever been put upon paper. But this, very naturally, she herself did not see. She went about at home on the quiet farm, filling every scrap of paper she could lay her hands on with verse and prose, with plays and romances. When she wasn't writing, she sat and waited for success. And success was to consist in this: some stranger who was very learned and influential, through some rare freak of fortune, was to come and discover what she had written and find it worth printing. After that, all the rest would come of itself.

Meanwhile nothing of the sort happened. And when the girl had passed her twentieth year, she began to grow impatient. She wondered why success did not come her way. Perhaps she lacked knowledge. She probably needed to see a little more of the world than the homestead in Värmland. And seeing that it would be a long time before she could earn her livelihood as an author, it was necessary for her to learn something—find some work in life—that she might have bread while she waited for herself. Or maybe it was simply this—that the story had lost patience with her. Perhaps it thought thus: "Since this blind person does not see that which lies nearest her eyes, let her be forced to go away. Let her tramp upon gray stone streets; let her live in cramped city rooms with no other outlook than gray stone walls; let her live among people who hide everything that is unusual in them and who appear to be all alike. It may, perchance, teach her to see that which is waiting outside the gate of her home—all that lives and moves between the stretch of blue hills which she has everyday before her eyes."

And so, one autumn, when she was twenty-two, she travelled up to Stockholm to begin preparing herself for the vocation of teacher.

The girl soon became absorbed in her work. She wrote no more, but went in for studies and lectures. It actually looked as though the story would lose her altogether.

Then something extraordinary happened. This same autumn, after she had been living a couple of months amidst gray streets and house walls, one day she was walking up Malmskillnad Street with a bundle of books under her arm. She had just come from a lecture on the history of literature. The lecture must have been about Bellman and Runeberg, because she was thinking of them and of the characters that live in their verses. She said to herself that Runeberg's jolly warriors and Bellman's happy-go-lucky roisterers were the very best material a writer could have to work with. And suddenly this thought flashed upon her: Värmland, the world in which you have been living, is not less remarkable than that of Fredman or Fanrik. If you can only learn how to handle it, you will find that your material is quite as good as theirs.

This is how it happened that she caught her first glimpse of the story, and the instant she saw it, the ground under her seemed to sway. The whole long Malmskillnad Street, from Hamn Street Hill to the firehouse, rose toward the skies and sank again—rose and sank. She stood still a long while, until the street had settled itself. She gazed with astonishment at the passers-by, who walked calmly along, apparently oblivious to the miracle that had taken place.

At that moment the girl determined that she would write the story of Värmland's Cavaliers, and never for an instant did she relinquish the thought of it, but many and long years elapsed before the determination was carried out.

In the first place, she had entered upon a new field of labor, and she lacked the time needful for the carrying out of a great literary work. In the second place, she had failed utterly in her first attempts to write the story.

During these years many things were constantly happening which helped mould it. One morning, on a school holiday, she was sitting at the breakfast table with her father, and the two of them talked of old times. Then he began telling of an acquaintance of his youth, whom he described as the most fascinating of men. This man brought joy and cheer with him wherever he went. He could sing; he composed music; he improvised verse. If he struck up a dance, it was not alone the young folk who danced, but old men and old women, high and low. If he made a speech, one had to laugh or cry, whichever he wished. If he drank himself full, he could play and talk better than when he was sober, and when he fell in love with a woman, it was impossible for her to resist him. If he did foolish things, one forgave him; if he was sad at times, one wanted to do anything and everything to see him glad again. But any great success in life he had never had, despite his wealth of talents. He had lived mostly at the foundries in Värmland as private tutor. Finally he was ordained as a minister. This was the highest that he had attained.

After this conversation, she could see the hero of her story better than heretofore, and with this a little life and action came into it. One fine day a name was given to the hero, and he was called Gösta Berling. Whence he got the name she never knew. It was as if he had named himself.

Another time, she came home to spend the Christmas holidays. One evening the whole family went off to a Christmas party, a good distance from home in a terrible blizzard. It turned out to be a longer drive than one would have thought. The horse plowed his way ahead at a walking pace. For several hours, she sat there in the sleigh in the blinding snowstorm and thought of the story. When they arrived finally, she had thought out her first chapter. It was the one about the Christmas night at the smithy.

What a chapter! It was her first, and for many years her only one. It was first written in verse, for the original plan was that it should be a romance cycle like "Fänrik Stål's Sagas." But by degrees this was changed, and for a time the idea was that it should be written as drama. Then the Christmas night was worked over to go in as the

155

first act. But this attempt did not succeed either; at last she decided to write the story as a novel. Then the chapter was written in prose. It grew enormously long, covering forty written pages. The last time it was rewritten it took up only nine.

After a few more years, came a second chapter. It was the story of the Ball at Borg and of the wolves that hunted Gösta Berling and Anna Stjernhök.

In the beginning this chapter was not written with the thought that it could come into the story, but as a sort of chance composition to be read at a small social gathering. The reading, however, was postponed, and the novelette was sent to *Dagny*. After a time, the story was returned as unacceptable for the magazine; in reality, it wasn't acceptable anywhere. As yet, it was altogether lacking in artistic smoothness.

Meanwhile, the author wondered to what purpose this unluckily born novella could be turned. Should she put it into the story? To be sure, it was an adventure by itself — and ended. It would look odd among the rest, which were better connected. Perhaps it wouldn't be such a bad idea, she thought, then, if all the chapters of the story were like this one—almost finished adventures? This would be difficult to carry out, but it might possibly be done. There would doubtless be gaps in the continuity here and there, but that should give the book great strength and variety.

Now, two important matters were settled: the story was to be a novel, and each chapter should be complete in itself. But nothing much had been gained hereby. She who had been fired with the idea of writing the story of Värmland's Cavaliers when she was twenty-two, at this stage was nearing the thirties and had not been able to write more than two chapters. Where had the years gone? She had graduated from the Teachers' College, and for several years past, had been a teacher at Landskrona. She had become interested in much and had been occupied with many things, but the story was just as unwritten. A mass of material had certainly been collected, but why was it so hard for her to write it down? Why did the inspiration never come to her? Why did the pen glide so slowly over the paper? She certainly had her dark moments at that time! She began to think that she never would finish her novel. She was that servant who buried his talent in the ground and never tried to use it.

As a matter of fact, all this occurred during the eighties, when stern Realism was at its height. She admired the great masters of that time, never thinking that one could use any other style in writing than the one they employed. For her own part, she liked the Romanticists better, but Romanticism was dead, and she was hardly the one to think of reviving its form and expression! Although her brain was filled to overflowing with stories of ghosts and mad love, of wondrously beautiful women and adventure-loving cavaliers, she tried to write about it in calm, realistic prose. She was not very clear-visioned. Another would have seen that the impossible was impossible.

Once she wrote a couple of chapters in another style. One was a scene from Svartsjö churchyard; the other was about the old philosopher, Uncle Eberhard and his infidel manuscripts. She scribbled them mostly in fun, with many ohs and ahs in the prose, which made it almost rhythmical. She perceived that in this vein she could write. There was inspiration in this—she could feel it. But when the two short chapters were finished, she laid them aside. They were only written in fun. One could not write a whole book in that vein.

But now the story had been waiting long enough. It thought, no doubt, as it did at the time when it sent her out in the world: "Again I must send this blinded person a great longing which will open her eyes."

The longing came over her in this manner; the homestead where she had grown up was sold. She journeyed to the home of her childhood to see it once again before strangers should occupy it.

157

The evening before she left there, perhaps nevermore to see the dear old place, she concluded in all meekness and humility to write the book in her own way and according to her own poor abilities. It was not going to be any great masterwork, as she had hoped. It might be a book at which people would laugh, but anyway she would write it—write it for herself, to save for herself what she could still save of the home—the dear old stories, the sweet peace of the carefree days, and the beautiful landscape with the long lakes and the many-hued blue hills.

But for her, who had hoped that she might yet learn to write a book people would care to read, it seemed as though she had relinquished the very thing in life she had been most eager to win. It was the hardest sacrifice she had made thus far.

A few weeks later, she was again at her home in Landskrona, seated at her writing desk. She began writing—she didn't know exactly what it was to be, but she was not going to be afraid of the strong words, the exclamations, the interrogations, nor would she be afraid to give herself with all her childishness and all her dreams! After she had come to this decision, the pen began to move almost by itself. This made her quite delirious. She was carried away with enthusiasm. Ah, this was writing! Unfamiliar thoughts and things, or, rather, things she never had surmised were stored away in her brain, crowded down upon the paper. The pages were filled with a haste of which she had never dreamed. What had hitherto required months—no, years—to work out, was now accomplished in a couple of hours. That evening, she wrote the story of the young countess's tramp over the ice on River Loven and the flood at Ekeby.

The following afternoon, she wrote the scene in which the gouty ensign, Rutger von Örneclou, tries to raise himself in bed to dance the Cachuca, and the evening of the next day, there appeared the story of the old mamsell who went off to visit the parsimonious Broby clergyman.

Now she knew for certain that in this style, she could write the book, but she was just as certain that no one would have the patience to read it through.

However, not many chapters let themselves be written like this—in one breath. Most of them required long and arduous labor, and there were only little snatches of time in the afternoons which she could devote to authorship. When she had been writing about half a year, reckoning from the day when she had gone in for Romanticism with a vengeance, about a dozen chapters were written. At this rate the book would be finished in three or four years.

It was in the spring of this year, 1890, that *Idun* invited prize competitors to send in short novellas of about one-hundred printed pages. This was an outlet for a story that wanted to be told and sent into the world. It must have been the story itself that prompted her sister to suggest to her that she make use of this opportunity. Here, at last, was a way of finding out if her story was so hopelessly bad! If it received the prize, much would be gained; if it didn't, she simply stood in exactly the same position as before.

She had nothing against the idea, but she had so little faith in herself that she couldn't come to any conclusion.

Finally, just eight days before the time for submitting manuscripts had expired, she decided to take five chapters from the novel, which were sufficiently well connected to pass for a novella, and chance it with these. But the chapters were far from ready. Three of them were loosely written, but of the remaining two there was barely an outline. Then the whole thing must be legibly copied, of course. To add to this, she was not at home just then, but was visiting her sister and brother-in-law, who still lived in Värmland. And one who has come to visit with dear friends for a short time cannot spend the days at a writing desk. She wrote, therefore, at night—sitting up the whole week until four in the mornings.

Finally there were only twenty-four hours of precious time left, and there were still twenty pages to be written.

On this, the last day, they were invited out. The whole family was going on a little journey—to be gone for the night. Naturally, she had to accompany the rest. When the party was over and the guests dispersed, she sat up all night writing in the strange place.

At times she felt very queer. The place where she was visiting was the very estate on which the wicked Sintram had lived. Fate, in a singular way, had brought her there on the very night when she must write about him who sat in the rocker and rocked.

Now and then, she looked up from her work and listened in the direction of the drawing room for the possible sound of a pair of rockers in motion. But nothing was heard. When the clock struck six the next morning, the five chapters were finished.

Along in the forenoon, they travelled home on a little freight steamer. There her sister did up the parcel, sealed it with sealing-wax, which had been brought from home for this purpose, wrote the address, and sent off the novella.

This happened on one of the last days in July. Toward the end of August, *Idun* contained a notice to the effect that something over twenty manuscripts had been received by the editors, but that one or two among them were so confusedly written they could not be counted in.

Then she gave up waiting for results. She knew, of course, which novella was so confusedly written that it could not be counted in.

One afternoon in November she received a curious telegram. It contained simply the words: "Hearty Congratulations," and was signed by three of her college classmates.

For her, it was a terribly long wait until dinner time of the following day, when the Stockholm papers were distributed. When the paper was in her hands, she had to search long without finding anything. Finally, on the last page, she found a little notice in fine print which told that

160

the prize had been awarded to her.

To another it might not have meant so much, perhaps, but for her it meant that she could devote herself to the calling which she had longed to follow all her life.

There is but little to add to this: the story that wanted to be told and sent out in the world was now fairly near its destination. Now it was to be written, at least, even though it might take a few years more before it was finished.

She, who was writing it, had gone up to Stockholm around Christmas time, after she had received the prize.

The editor of *Idun* volunteered to print the book as soon as it was finished.

If she could ever find time to write it!

The evening before she was to return to Landskrona, she spent with her loyal friend, Baroness Adlersparre, to whom she read a few chapters aloud.

"Esselde"[1] listened, as only she could listen, and she became interested. After the reading, she sat silently and pondered. "How long will it be before all of it is ready?" she asked finally.

"Three or four years." Then they parted.

The next morning, two hours before she was to leave Stockholm, a message came from Esselde bidding her to come before her departure.

The old Baroness was in her most positive and determined mood. "Now you must take a leave of absence for a year and finish the book. I shall procure the money."

Fifteen minutes later, the girl was on her way to the principal of the Teachers' College to ask her assistance in securing a substitute.

At one o'clock, she was happily seated in the railway carriage. But now she was going no farther than Sörmland, where she had good friends who lived in a charming villa.

[1]Baroness Adlersparre—pen name, Esselde—was a noted Swedish writer, publisher, and philanthropist, and a contemporary of Fredrika Bremer.

And so they, Otto Gumaelius and his wife, gave her the freedom of their home—freedom to work, and peace, and the best of care for nearly a year until the book was finished.

Now, at last, she could write from morning till night. It was the happiest time of her life.

But when the story was finished at the close of the summer, it looked queer. It was wild and disordered, and the connecting threads were so loose that all the parts seemed bent upon following their old inclination to wander off, each in its own way.

It never became what it should have been.

Its misfortune was that it had been compelled to wait so long to be told. If it was not properly disciplined and restrained, it was mostly because the author was so overjoyed in the thought that at last she had been privileged to write it.

Mårbacka, ancestral home of Selma Lagerlöf

CHRONOLOGY

1858	Selma Lagerlöf born, November 20, at Mårbacka in Värmland, Sweden.
1863	Grandmother, Lisa Maja Lagerlöf, dies.
1867	Visits Stockholm for treatment of lameness.
1873	Second visit to Stockholm, told in "The Stockholm Diary."
1882–1885	Studies at a teachers college for gifted women in Stockholm.
1885	Father dies.
1885–1895	Works as a teacher at a junior high school for girls in southern Sweden at Landskrona.
1888	Mårbacka sold.
1891	First novel, *Gösta Berling's Saga*, published.
1894	*Invisible Links*, a collection of stories.
1895–1896	Travel in Italy and Europe on a stipend from King Oscar II.
1897	Moves to Falun in the province of Dalecarlia.
1899	*Queens at Kungahälla*, stories about Scandinavian nobility.
1899–1900	Travel in Egypt and Palestine (now Israel).
1906–1907	*The Wonderful Adventures of Nils* and *The Further Adventures of Nils*, books originally commissioned by the government to teach schoolchildren Sweden's geography.
1907	Aunt Lovisa dies. Selma Lagerlöf purchases Mårbacka.
1908	*The Girl from the Marsh Croft*, stories.
1909	Wins the Nobel Prize for Literature.
1910	Purchases the entire estate surrounding Mårbacka and becomes an active landowner. Lives there during the summers.
1914	Becomes a member of the Swedish Academy.
1919	Begins to live year-round at Mårbacka.
1922	*Mårbacka*, first part of her memoirs.
1930	*Memories of My Childhood*.
1932	*The Diary of Selma Lagerlöf*.
1934	*Harvest*, a selection of short prose.
1940	Dies, March 16.

Sources:

Edström, Vivi. *Selma Lagerlöf*. Trans. Barbara Lide. Boston: Twayne Publishers, 1984.

Larsen, Hanna Astrup. *Selma Lagerlöf*. Garden City: Doubleday, Doran and Co., 1936.

Other Works by Selma Lagerlöf

Christ Legends
The Emperor of Portugallia
The Girl from the Marsh Croft
Gösta Berling's Saga
Harvest
Jerusalem
Liliecrona's Home
Miracles of the Antichrist
Queens of Kungahälla and other Sketches
The Ring of the Löwenskölds
The Tale of a Manor
The Treasure

Autobiographical writings
  Mårbacka
  Memories of my Childhood: Further
    Years at Mårbacka
  The Diary of Selma Lagerlöf

Children's stories
  The Wonderful Adventures of Nils
  The Further Adventures of Nils